Bill-

Im so grateful to God for our friendship, and for bringing us together for this great enterprise!

Phil

INSIDE COLLEGE MERGERS

INSIDE
COLLEGE
MERGERS

Stories from the Front Lines

Edited by
MARK LA BRANCHE

JOHNS HOPKINS UNIVERSITY PRESS | *Baltimore*

© 2024 Johns Hopkins University Press
All rights reserved. Published 2024
Printed in the United States of America on acid-free paper

2 4 6 8 9 7 5 3 1

Johns Hopkins University Press
2715 North Charles Street
Baltimore, Maryland 21218
www.press.jhu.edu

Library of Congress Cataloging-in-Publication Data
Names: La Branche, Mark, 1958– editor.
Title: Inside college mergers : stories from the front lines /
Edited by Mark La Branche.
Description: Baltimore, Maryland : Johns Hopkins University Press, 2024. |
Includes bibliographical references and index.
Identifiers: LCCN 2023029965 | ISBN 9781421448602 (hardcover) |
ISBN 9781421448619 (ebook)
Subjects: LCSH: Universities and colleges—Mergers—United States. |
Mission statements—United States.
Classification: LCC LB2341 .M398 2024 | DDC 378.1/040973—dc23/eng/20230825
LC record available at https://lccn.loc.gov/2023029965

A catalog record for this book is available from the British Library.

Special discounts are available for bulk purchases of this book.
For more information, please contact Special Sales at specialsales@jh.edu.

CONTENTS

ACKNOWLEDGMENTS

I would like to express my deepest gratitude to the courageous leaders who agreed to generously share their institutional stories from their unique perspectives. Together, we express our sincere appreciation for the heroic work of the faculty, staff, and trustees that these stories represent.

INSIDE COLLEGE MERGERS

Introduction

SINCE THE EARLY 2000S, the United States has been experiencing a substantial season of disruption, and higher education institutions expect to feel the effects of that disruption for many years to come. It was already predicted that the number of high school graduates in the United States would sharply decrease in 2025 due to a birth dearth during the Great Recession. Both disruptions are bound to hasten an already declining college-going rate. At the same time, the necessity of postsecondary education has never been greater as we respond to the needs of an increasingly complex world. Disruptions such as widespread questioning of the value proposition of a four-year degree and the growing number of states offering tuition-free options will critically challenge the private college and university business model. Institutions are dealing with these disruptions as expansions in the accessibility, affordability, and quality of online certification and degree programs are changing the landscape of higher education. The good news is that while disruptions are nothing new to higher education leaders, neither is adaptation.

Historically, institutions have demonstrated a remarkable resilience and ability to adapt to changing circumstances and a changing world. What is new about the world of higher education administration is that the pace of change has increased exponentially, requiring a new level of agility and urgency. The incremental strategies that served us well in the past are not likely to allow us to catch up with or get ahead of these accelerating, challenging trends. The pace of change will require a strong proactive stance that deliberately, purposely, and prospectively meets the challenges and opportunities before us. A reactive posture would certainly keep us busy and may result in some small wins that possibly buy us some time, but ultimately it will not increase our pace of adaptation. One major truth to be learned from the stories in this book is that the best time to adapt is when the elements of our circumstances are not forcing us into a reactive stance. We do not have to miss a payroll, suspend the pension match program, or fail to comply with the principles of accreditation to create a burning platform from which to leap. While a serious crisis can force open the aperture of our vision to see new possibilities, so too can the disciplined and steady force that comes with a culture of urgent preparedness.

The seven stories included in this book are firsthand profiles of institutions that took a leap in their thinking and acting. Each process is unique. Each was precipitated by different circumstances, entered into with different visions of success, and ended with different outcomes. Each story is a testament to the importance of making mission primary and having the will to preserve it.

While a leap suggests a sudden move, the factors that brought about the need to change were mounting over a number of years. In the case of St. Andrews University, loss of accreditation was the driving force in seeking a partnership that would maintain its identity and preserve its mission. Wesley College faced dire financial headwinds that could no longer be ameliorated. They sought to preserve the campus for the sake of the Dover community and in order to continue to provide access for students. Iowa Wesleyan University had announced its possible closure prior to the failure of its effort to establish a merger partner. It then reexamined its mission and created new partnerships that brought benefit to its community and enrollment growth. And while the partnerships were a success, it would not be enough to sustain IWU long term. Montreat College experienced years of financial struggle and a failed attempt to merge before an extraordinary gift provided a lifeline, allowing the college and its leadership to focus on the hard work of transformational change that would lead to a more sustainable future. For Roosevelt University and Robert Morris University, proximity, existing partnerships, and a shared mission led to integration. At Wheelock College, facing an inevitable closure, leaders sought to ensure a healthy end that ultimately preserved the mission and honored the legacy of the school. Boston University provided Wheelock with an alternative future that would do both. Martin Methodist College was surviving on the thinnest of margins when the COVID-19 pandemic brought issues of sustainability into clear focus. The college leadership needed to think beyond identity and traditional operational strategies in order to secure and expand its mission. When the possibility of becoming the fourth undergraduate campus of the University of Tennessee system presented itself, it was an idea whose time had come.

Two of the institutions profiled in this book entered a strategic merger process that did not result in an acquisition. However, the experiences opened those institutions to what is referred to by Iowa Wesleyan University in chapter 3 as an "alternative future." The merger process, even when ended before acquisition, can lead to a renewed sense of mission and purpose, new ways of operating, and previously undiscovered partnerships that help sustain and expand the mission of both institutions.

In this book and in higher education, the term *merger* is used as a general identifier of any number of ways that two or more institutions come together to share resources and capacity to create efficiencies. One example of this generalization is the consolidation of institutions within a larger system, such as can be found recently in the Georgia and Pennsylvania systems. Another example is St. Andrews University, which remained a separate corporate entity but formed a partnership and became a branch campus of Webber International University for purposes of accreditation. Readers will also notice that the terms *merger* and *acquisition* are often used interchangeably. All of the completed mergers described in this book are technically acquisitions, where one partner ends up with the balance of power. Acquisition does not involve an exchange of money but the transfer of assets and particular liabilities to the acquiring institution. This is all done through terms of agreement that outline expectations and requirements for the transfer of assets. A merger as the acquisition of an institution by another institution can take on a variety of forms. For example, (1) one institution is absorbed by another without maintaining its identity but continues its program and mission; (2) the facilities of an institution are acquired by another institution as an extension of its campus, preserving the place of the institution in the community and maintaining some elements of its mission; (3) one institution is acquired by another while maintaining its identity and mission; or (4) one institution is acquired by another and changes its identity but maintains its mission and autonomy.

While each chapter author has a unique story to tell, they all share lessons that will serve as a reference to any college that is contemplating merger, acquisition, or partnership as a strategic tool in order to preserve, expand, and sustain its mission. Beyond the tactical information to be gleaned from this book, it also contains a trove of lessons in leadership and leadership philosophy. The contributors to this book hope that their experiences, both personally and institutionally, will be a valuable resource to you as you help steward the mission of the institution you serve.

CHAPTER ONE

Honoring Legacy and Preserving Mission

MARY L. CHURCHILL

Vice President, Academic Affairs, Wheelock College

Associate Dean of Strategic Initiatives and Community Engagement,
Boston University

THE FUTURE FOR HUNDREDS OF small colleges in this country is predicted by higher education futurists to be chaotic and messy. I know that firsthand. Together with its last president, David Chard, and its board of trustees, I helped guide one of those financially precarious institutions— Wheelock College in Boston—to close, after wrestling with the available options. In doing so we merged Wheelock with a larger institution, preserved its mission, and honored its legacy. In the case of Wheelock College, that mission was improving the lives of children and families.

This is a personal story of how we led our college to a healthy end, and how we developed as leaders along the way. Above all, I want to share this story to help other college leaders navigate their own troubled waters. For those seeking texts that assume a more traditional academic approach to university mergers, I recommend pairing this story with two important works: *Strategic Mergers in Higher Education* by Ricardo Azziz and colleagues (2019) and *Consolidating Colleges and Merging Universities: New Strategies for Higher Education Leaders* by James Martin and James E. Samuels & Associates (2017).

Closing a college can be a disaster. The legacy and mission can simply fade away, with jobs eliminated, buildings sold, and students left to fend for themselves. I don't believe that this outcome is inevitable. When considered and executed thoughtfully, closing a college can preserve an essential element of its institutional character: the work it does for society.

After helping to shepherd the merger of Wheelock College with Boston University (BU) in 2018, I have had some time to reflect. First, I would like to emphasize that I tell this story from my own point of view. I was the vice president for academic affairs at Wheelock and am now an administrator in Boston University's Wheelock College of Education and Human Development. (An extended exploration of the Wheelock/ Boston University merger is the subject of the book *When Colleges Close: Leading in a Time of Crisis*, which I coauthored with David Chard.) While I try to represent the many points of view of those affected by this merger and closure, this is not the same story that faculty, staff, students, alumni, or trustees would relate.

As a first-generation college student, I have long known that student experiences and outcomes are the front line for equity in higher education, so I have often chosen roles and institutions that would put me in a position to serve BIPOC and first-generation students. Many of these students can be found in professional studies divisions, which I led at Northeastern University and Salem State University, where I worked with community college partners through transfer summits, early college initiatives, and other innovative partnerships. I represented Salem State in the Boston Foundation's Success Boston initiative and worked with other nonprofits in communities of color that coached students through the application process to the completion of a four-year college degree.

So, I came to Wheelock with many years of higher education experience as a faculty member, academic administrator, and as dean in both public and private institutions of diverse sizes.

I have committed my career to higher education, which I would not have done had I not believed deeply in its power. I believe in personal and public investment in higher education; creating access and empowering individuals to reach their full potential through higher education is the mark of a successful, democratic society.

Today's higher education landscape is remarkably different from the one that greeted me when I began my career in the late 1980s. In a 2016 report about the past fifty years of the sector, the current period in higher education is referred to as the "third era." The first, "expansion," ran from 1968 to 1990, and the second, "transformed by technology," ran from 1991 to 2010. This so-called third era is marked by contraction: a significant demographic shift, fewer high school graduates, reduced financial support at the state and federal levels, and rising tuition costs (EY-Parthenon 2016, 2).

In this era of contraction, nearly every risk factor you can imagine pertained to Wheelock College. The college focused on training teachers and social workers, which meant that few of its alumni were wealthy. It was in New England, a region that faced the most significant demographic changes in the United States. Some predicted a drop of more than 15% in students who would pursue a college degree (Grawe 2018). Wheelock students were of traditional college age, 18–22 years, and lived on campus—precisely the profile of an institution poised to face strong headwinds. Many small colleges find themselves at particular risk, because they are less competitive than large, well-endowed institutions, and while they tend to recruit regionally in areas most impacted by demographic changes, they may also be less able to pivot quickly to meet market demands.

To deliver strong college and career pathways, higher education, government, business, and philanthropy need to collaborate on vision, programs, and strategies to meet the needs of all students. Leading up to Wheelock's closure, the Great Recession of 2008 forced students and their families to reconsider the value of a college degree when its cost, and the associated debt, would engender ongoing financial distress. The media was full of reports about the costs of higher education, the exceptions—those who had achieved phenomenal success as dropouts (Bill Gates, Michael Dell)—and millennial graduates, back at home, unemployed and dependent on family support. Higher education deserves more nuanced and multifocal reporting from corporate media.

The COVID-19 pandemic created an entire array of new challenges, all of which place small, non-elite, liberal arts schools in a perpetual struggle. To survive, some may have to reinvent themselves in ways that may not reflect their traditional missions and legacies. At Wheelock, that mission was to serve children and families, and it was not reduced to saving the institution at any cost. The trustees, half of whom were Wheelock alumni, were sensitive to sustaining the college's mission. Anything less was unacceptable. They cared so much about this that one option they considered, if the college could not be saved, was to close, liquidate the assets, and create a foundation.

Some might ask, Why would you and David Chard be willing to jump into what observers saw as "serious trouble"? The reason was that we both thought we could help preserve the college's mission and legacy. We embraced uncertainty while having no idea what form that mission would take.

Colleges are decentralized institutions with complicated webs of interconnected constituencies and sources of power. Higher education leadership deserves special attention. My experience gave me the opportunity to explore some of the leadership theories I'd been exposed to in the past. One belief within higher education is that college administrators should engage in "servant leadership," in service to students, the mission, or the faculty. Another theory is that administrators should provide "authentic leadership," which Walumbwa, Lawler, and Avolio (2007) refer to as leadership that elevates self-awareness, relational transparency, a highly internalized moral perspective, and balanced processing—that is, seeking out different points of view before decision-making takes place.

I cannot say whether our leadership team adhered to one theory or the other, or a combination of both, but we kept the following in mind throughout the full course of Wheelock's transition: we sought to offer transparency, self-awareness, shared decision-making, multiple communication channels, open listening sessions, and the frequent admission that we did not have or know all the answers.

Some of the qualities of authentic leadership are open communication, intellectual humility, and honesty. While we did not characterize our actions in that way at the time, in retrospect we see that the board and leadership team at Wheelock during the period spanning the merger and closure were often exemplary. Larger than any individual ego was a shared goal to uphold the integrity of Wheelock's original mission and legacy, which in turn inspired leaders to demonstrate the qualities that embody authentic leadership in order to achieve positive outcomes.

Moreover, an institution facing financial challenges and life-changing transitions requires leadership that is more than transactional. It requires leaders who understand the institution's place within a larger frame, who communicate honestly and transparently, and honor the institution's history.

In times of upheaval and significant change, it is important for leaders to know how their institutions stand and to ask themselves, What makes sense for this institution right now? To know and respect the history of an institution in view of its best interests, one needs to identify the institutional historians, those who carry the culture of a place, such as prominent alumni, emeritus faculty, and key cultural representatives at the institution. New leaders need to get to know them and to respect their knowledge and contribution. It is sometimes the case that leaders who face an existential crisis do not give these individuals sufficient attention, or try to work around them, as if they were impediments to progress. They do this at their peril. I recommend that leaders create both official and unofficial advisory boards composed of those with deep knowledge and appreciation for the institution, and that leaders listen, understand, and respect all those who have brought the institution to this current point in its history.

During the process of merging and closing, it seemed imperative that we tie Wheelock's past to its future—connecting the next era (whatever form that might take) to the history of the college. In highlighting the college's history, we were able to show how change had always been a part of the institution's essential activity. Lucy Wheelock's initial goals, for instance, were not to create a four-year college but a flexible model that might adapt to changes brought on by the society in which the school found itself.

A college degree is one of the best ways to ensure financial independence and success—even better health—over the course of one's life. If degrees did not hold such value, we would not fight to ensure that populations historically denied access to higher education—women, first-generation students, and students of color—are able to attend college. Negative messages in our popular culture continue to undercut the value of college in a manner that obscures the real advantages of a degree, not only to individuals but also to society. The demographic decline of high school students in the Northeast and Upper Midwest over the subsequent generation, as illustrated by Nathan Grawe (2018), has created a severe downturn in enrollment for many institutions. Small, non-elite institutions are among the hardest hit.

Strategies to counter these trends have included diversified academic programming, an expansion into online and international markets, and the development of a particular niche that includes market-driven programs to attract students, such as business concentrations or the health profession. A robust endowment can also make a considerable difference. Institutions able to save themselves from dramatic financial decline are in the minority. Wheelock College did not have much to weather its financial challenges. In 2015, its endowment was around $45 million. For comparison, there are about six hundred colleges in the United States with larger endowments, including roughly one hundred that top $1 billion. Boston University, for instance, has an endowment of more than $2 billion. A small, but comparatively rich, college like Oberlin College and Conservatory boasts an endowment of around $900 million. Consider that the annual interest on such a sum is greater than Wheelock's entire endowment (Chronicle of Higher Education 2019).

A rough timeline of the conditions and actions that led to Wheelock's search for a partner institution follows. Undergraduate enrollment at Wheelock had been on the rise for a few years but peaked in 2015 at approximately 1,200 undergraduates and 400 graduates, short of the 2,000 students the college estimated it would need to sustain its financial independence. Wheelock trustees believed that New England would experience a dramatic demographic shift, and that if the college did not adapt to diversify its student base—traditionally composed of residential 18-year-old undergraduates—enrollment would continue to erode.

At Wheelock, the trustees were properly concerned about the future and saw that extreme tuition discounting would have a negative impact on the college's finances. In 2013, Kate Taylor, the chair of the board of trustees, requested a financial model that would project the college's balance sheet for at least five years. She—and at least some of her fellow trustees—found the results alarming. Others were more optimistic and felt that by investing in marketing and recruitment, enrollments would climb and the financial future of the college would improve. The challenges posed by the five-year model were tabled, because college leadership had far more pressing issues: the campus was faced with faculty and student unrest, a lack of consistent academic leadership, a wave of negative press coverage, and an upcoming accreditation visit. Moreover, the college was running a surplus. Long-range financial health did not rise to the top of the list.

The Wheelock trustees saw that many students and families could not afford the rising tuition rates. Wheelock had been successful in attracting students of color, often first-generation college students with significant financial need. Like many institutions, Wheelock offered discounted tuition fees to attract and retain these families. When enrollment began to drop off in 2012, a decline in tuition revenue forced the college to cut costs, notably staff expenses.

Other small colleges had diversified academic offerings, in a move to respond to market demand, in fields such as health care, business, and technology. Wheelock continued to focus on its legacy: teaching, early childhood development, and social work with a strong and diverse arts and sciences curriculum. While professional academic areas were central to the mission of Wheelock College, enrollment continued to decline in these areas nationwide. Local institutions such as Simmons College (now Simmons University) added online curricula to expand impact and increase gross tuition revenue. By contrast in 2016–17, Wheelock inched forward with an online curriculum, offering only one graduate certificate in STEM teaching.

While the board of trustees was intent on maintaining independence, they were equally focused on adhering to the college's original mission: to improve the lives of children and families. What could that mean in the twenty-first century? To provide a wider range of services—and to do so affordably—had been at the center of the college's decision to join the Colleges of the Fenway consortium. This group, formed in 1998, brought together six colleges in the center of Boston, including

Simmons College and the Wentworth Institute of Technology. The consortium repaid real benefits for Wheelock such as reduced insurance costs and enhanced purchasing power. However, the goal of creating a robust set of shared academic programs never materialized.

Frequent changes in leadership prevented the creation of new academic programs. Between 2004 and 2016, six different vice presidents for academic affairs at Wheelock arrived and departed. Persistent turnover made sustained change impossible. This trend, turnover in the chief academic officer role, had been increasing across the United States, with a median tenure of just less than four years (American Council of Education, n.d.; Jaschik and Lederman 2019). A lack of consistent leadership posed a real challenge for academic collaboration among the consortium's member institutions. When I assumed the role of vice president for academic affairs at Wheelock in July 2017, three of the six Fenway institutions had interim provosts.

Added to academic and financial challenges, morale on campus was poor. Black Lives Matter student protests were taking place on many US campuses in the 2015–16 academic year, and Wheelock's students were also making demands of the administration. Students of color and their allies voiced concerns about how they were treated in the classroom by some faculty. College leadership invited the Black-Jew Dialogues, a touring comedy duo known for parodying prejudices of both identities to promote strength in diversity, to campus. Several Jewish faculty members signed a letter registering their concern about not being consulted before the event was scheduled, and two of those members subsequently lodged a complaint with the federal Equal Employment Opportunity Commission, charging that Wheelock's leadership had targeted them with antisemitic bias. Students and professors argued that the college was not doing enough to address racial bias.

In the spring of 2015, Wheelock's accreditor—the New England Association of Schools and Colleges (NEASC)—issued a confidential report on the state of the college's health. It noted concerns about the lack of consistent academic leadership and struggles with shared governance. While not a glowing report, it was not out of the ordinary for a small college. However, a story that ran in the *Boston Globe* characterized the report as an exposé, and not as what it was, as an ordinary accreditation review, and the reporter emphasized that the college faced "financial challenges, an upheaval from overburdened faculty, and fallout from an exodus of top staff" (Krantz 2015). From the *Globe's* perspective, Wheelock College was in a fragile position.

By early 2016, Wheelock's situation had become complicated, to say the least. The president was planning to retire at the end of the school year, enrollment was in decline, the budget was in the red, and tensions between faculty, administrators, and the board of trustees were growing. While some of the negative publicity was the result of careless reporting in the *Boston Globe*, there was no denying that the reputation of the college had taken a hit. Wheelock's trustees knew that they needed a new president who could quickly build trust. They needed someone who would be a good listener, who had a history of being honest and transparent and who also had suitable academic credentials for Wheelock. They needed candidates who were innovative and entrepreneurial, and who could present them with an array of possibilities and options– no matter how radical—to lead the college into its future.

As the board prepared to search for President Jackie Jenkins-Scott's replacement, the trustees became increasingly concerned about the college's finances. A potential partnership or, even more radical, a merger became a serious consideration. Many trustees believed that the college could not go it alone. In 2015, after the president had publicly announced her plan to retire in June 2016, the Wheelock College Board of Trustees approached a local institution about the possibility of forming a partnership (the name of the institution must remain anonymous owing to nondisclosure agreements). This led to explorations, by a board task force, of a potential partnership with that institution or others. But leadership struggles continued to hamper these negotiations. Given her imminent departure, President Jenkins-Scott did not wish to participate in conversations about a merger. Consequently, the board involved the chief financial officer without the president, and as yet, Wheelock had no provost.

The trustees were divided on seeking a merger. A few felt that they needed to be bold and public, while others felt that exploring a merger was premature. The merger debate became contentious, and there was even fear that a small group of trustees would "sell the college."

The board then hired a consultant to help them navigate the landscape of higher education mergers. The news was not good. Plenty of merger partners existed, in theory, but they looked a lot like Wheelock— small, private colleges, struggling financially. Why join forces with another college in the same boat? They needed to find a different boat altogether. The consultant reviewed the landscape but could not recommend a specific direction. In essence, the opinion was, "This is uncharted territory."

At the same time, the board began a search for the next president but did not tell the search firm that a merger was a real possibility. The trustees knew this was untenable. How could they find a new president for an institution that might not be around much longer? The task force gave itself a deadline. By January 16, 2016, just a few weeks hence, they had to pick one of three options: scrap the search and move forward with a merger partner, hire an interim president, or continue the search for a new president.

After another contentious meeting in mid-January, the board chose the third option, but with a twist. They would move ahead with the presidential search, suspend the merger discussions for the time being, and add clarity to the job description for the new president: "continue and extend conversations with potential strategic partners, with all options on the table from specific collaborations up to and including consolidation or merger." This last decision made their intentions far more transparent than before. Candidates would know what they were getting into, but would there be any candidates? The search firm was concerned that all the "good" candidates would fade away. An interim president would be the only option. After contacting all of the semifinalists to let them know how the job description had changed and that this would include exploring the possibility of a job that might not exist in the future, the chair of the search committee—contrary to the search firm's concern—was able to confirm that all candidates chose to stay in the running.

Of the three final candidates invited to Wheelock's campus, David Chard was overwhelmingly the top choice on the part of trustees, faculty, students, and staff. The board hired David as the next and fourteenth president of Wheelock College. His immediate mandates were to work on admissions and faculty culture, and to hire a vice president for academic affairs. He believed he would be able to remedy and address the college's challenges and financial difficulties. To move the college forward, he understood, would require a careful examination of all academic programs, a reduction in unnecessary expenses, and market analysis to learn how Wheelock could grow in New England's competitive higher ed market. David was well aware that Wheelock had had a succession of vice presidents for academic affairs, and that academic leadership was a pressing need. An absence of continuity in leadership might explain, in part, a lack of coherence in academic planning.

While an air of excitement about the new leadership pervaded campus in the spring of 2016, it was still the case that trust had eroded between the trustees, the administration, and the faculty. The focus and energy of the leadership team was to regain that trust, to develop and implement transparent processes, to secure stability in the academic leadership positions, and to promote community healing.

In his first all-college meeting of 2016–17, on September 26, 2016, David shared budget and enrollment information with the full college community, which was the first time the full picture had been shared with them. This type of transparency can be a shock to the community. Reactions can range from disbelief and misunderstanding to confusion and anger and, finally, to resignation and a sense of guilt from those who feel responsible. How did this happen? How did we get here? Whose fault is this? Past presidents and boards are often blamed. Staff blame the faculty. Faculty blame the administration. Broader societal trends— often the core problem—rarely get the attention they deserve. Even well-meaning progressive faculty may think that a single leader is to blame or could have saved the college.

Against the turbulence of the 2016 presidential election result and increasing tension on campuses experienced by minorities and women with collective uncertainty about the country's future, Wheelock's board met in December: David recommended that the college create a faculty retirement incentive plan. The goal, he told the trustees, would be to reduce the number of senior faculty and staff by as many as fifteen individuals. This would not save money in the short term, he said. In fact, it would require cash from the college's reserves. However, the college would be leaner and better able to innovate. David told the board that this was the kind of decision required in preparation for change.

Toward the end of December, David also put together a cross-college search committee to help identify the next vice president for academic affairs. He hoped to find an academic leader with whom he could work closely, who had experience in making strategic changes and initiating program growth, someone preferably in New England. The job would include revitalizing programs, an understanding of the market, and careful investment in new programs that would attract students. David could not predict how the college would resolve the many issues it faced, or whether he would be able to attract a capable leader for this position. He wanted to make decisions that would have a positive impact on the college for years to come.

David reached out to me as well as others. I had the type of academic career that was possible in Boston—more than three decades of leadership roles at wildly different institutions: first at Northeastern University, and then at Salem State University. I had pushed for creative, revenue-generating programs and was, at that time, associate provost for innovation and partnerships and dean of graduate and professional programs. In our first conversation, David was blunt. He reviewed Wheelock's challenges, and, having experience in implementing disruptive change, I asked him if Wheelock was really open to change and wanted to know how much the school was willing to do. I felt I could help him assess the "enterprise value" of the institution while gauging the urgency with which leadership would need to undertake bold action. (I accepted David Chard's offer for the position early in April 2017, and my first day on the job was set for July 1, 2017.)

I have seen other small colleges struggle and recollect many of the feelings we experienced at Wheelock from 2016 to 2018. A board may become sharply divided as it succumbs to financial pressures, possible closure or a merger, and the problem of deciding what the best course of action may be. When a board is divided, the pursuit of any partnership is made more difficult. Unfortunately, colleges behave like families when they occasionally dysfunction. Wheelock's trustees were not immune to this challenge but took time to work through their disagreements, allowing themselves to learn about the chances of how they might best overcome the financial difficulties that plague so many small colleges. When they reached a consensus, they were motivated to be successful. The decision to hire a consulting firm in 2017, and for $500,000, was a litmus test for Wheelock. If the board had not been prepared to invest at that level for the future of the institution, they would not have been ready to pursue a merger. It was a significant financial investment that required a serious study of the college's financial resources. In some cases, an investment like this may require the liquidation of assets such as real estate. However, if a board is not prepared or unwilling to make this commitment, it is probably not ready to eliminate its own leadership positions.

Another litmus test might be a board's decision to hire leaders who are willing to go through with a merger or partnership. If both the board and leadership agree with respect to the pursuit of a partnership or merger, those efforts are more likely to succeed. Furthermore, Wheelock's board knew that their new president had to be able to innovate, take risks, and prioritize the future of the college over satisfaction of ego. As a caveat, in recent years, many institutional mergers have been thwarted by divided boards.

To sum up, declines in enrollment and financial challenges may be the ultimate reasons a college finds itself in significant trouble, but other factors such as internal and external relationships, academic health, and governance can make important contributions to future success. The challenges that lead to a college's ultimate closure do not occur suddenly. Instead, they build up over time, with additional challenges that may distract leadership from dealing with the more serious problems an institution faces. Communication, particularly information that reaches the public, must be managed carefully, since it can lead to perceptions that may impact the institution's enrollment, misrepresent the severity of some issues, and hasten closure. Trustees of most nonprofit higher education institutions are charged with making financial decisions and need to accept this responsibility and be courageous enough to take bold actions.

It is essential to educate members of a college community to understand their role in the business enterprise and financial health of a college. Transparency must be accompanied by regular progress updates and accountability. The board went on a retreat in March to discuss strategy and to reach consensus on steps going forward.

In April 2017, David invited proposals from three consulting firms with experience in higher education business and finance. Wheelock needed help to prepare itself to make bold decisions. The president and trustees chose Parthenon of Ernst & Young Global Limited (now EY-Parthenon), a Boston-based consulting firm that had helped with the 2016 merger of the School of the Museum of Fine Arts with Tufts University. The trustees had agreed to entertain radical change in hiring consultants. At this point in 2017, they also knew that some things were not up for debate. Any partnership had to preserve the Wheelock brand and mission. It had to keep the name and legacy of Lucy Wheelock alive. Additional nonnegotiable terms included the guarantee of continued support of students and alumni. Given the strength of Wheelock's history and brand, a partnership brought not only the preservation of Wheelock's mission but also amplification of its impact. The trustees remembered that there had been a time when the Wheelock name carried more weight and prestige than it did in 2017. Wheelock would also need to fund and hire legal support for any merger discussions, as well as an external communications firm to manage messaging and media. The college had skimped on crisis communications in the past, and leaders had seen the effects of the faculty discrimination lawsuits and plagiarism case levied against a former vice president for academic affairs.

The Real Estate Committee followed up with a recommendation to put the president's house and an adjacent residence hall on the market, and to sell both as is. David assured the trustees that his team would work with a realtor to identify the best way to list the real estate parcels, and that he would report back on ongoing developments. The initial valuation for both properties was $8 million. The board needed to get cash into the college's strategic account. One board member stressed, "Don't get greedy, get speedy." In other words, look for the best possible deal, but don't wait too long.

In the meantime, EY-Parthenon recommended creating a Strategic Options Committee (often referred to as the strategy committee) composed of a selection of trustees and administrators who reported regularly to the board. The committee was integral to EY-Parthenon's approach to strategic partnerships, and in the final result it was highly successful in Wheelock's merger with Boston University.

EY-Parthenon's approach to this project included internal data, market research and discussions with potential merger partners, and working sessions with institutional leadership. The trustees liked that EY-Parthenon's consultants were willing to move quickly; they proposed an aggressive timeline. Everyone agreed on a deadline to identify a solution by the fall of 2017, which was only twelve weeks away. The engagement began on April 24, 2017, and included three phases as follows:

> Phase 1 would be a one-week planning phase when the project would be launched, and members of the strategy committee would be identified. EY-Parthenon would facilitate a kick-off meeting with the committee to frame evaluation criteria, test the viability of possible solutions, narrow the set of stand-alone options to one or two of the most likely candidates, and validate the three institutions with which Wheelock College had already been in discussion, to confirm they might still be valid partners.
>
> Phase 2 would include the creation of a strategic option evaluation framework with a short list of options. This alone had a three-week timeline.
>
> Phase 3 included a merger process design, refinement of the evaluation rubric, and facilitation of board decision-making, all of which was projected to take five weeks.

EY-Parthenon pushed the strategy committee to define Wheelock's priorities, and in final agreement the most important items were (1) retaining Wheelock's' mission, name, and identity; (2) providing Wheelock's students with full access to the partner's offerings; and (3) maintaining Wheelock's coeducational status. The committee also agreed on a set of mid-level priorities that would be subject to negotiation, with a willingness to get one or two in place but not all. The mid-level priorities were as follows: (1) retaining a small school environment, (2) prioritizing representation on the board, and (3) maximizing employee retention.

Low-level priorities that would be nice to have but were not necessary included some of the following: (1) continuing to serve both undergraduate and graduate students; (2) retaining control over academic departments that were not core to the mission of the college and control over final admissions decisions and financial aid remaining in Boston; and (3) the ability to retain a residential aspect for students.

We learned from this process that it pays to begin early in strategic planning in order to identify the community's highest priorities or nonnegotiables. These should be thoroughly considered in light of the institution's history, mission, and future goals. Factors like real estate may, at first glance, feel nonnegotiable but become less important in the face of other more critical factors. Within the possibility of a strategic partnership or merger, an institution needs to make itself an attractive partner. This may involve reducing the number of full-time personnel or selling valuable properties, which themselves create an expense line.

It is best to be as honest as possible with faculty and staff with respect to the search for sustainable options, and when reviewing options for a sustainable future, it is critical that leaders test out each option for viability. After all the decisions are made, it is essential that all members of the Strategic Options Committee can articulate why a particular decision was made, instead of another. There were ultimately six vision proposals from six institutions, which were scored according to the criteria outlined by the Strategic Options Committee. All of their proposals were thoughtful, respectful of the non-negotiable priorities, and potentially viable alternatives. In fact, committee members frequently commented that we were fortunate that all options were good options, though some were better. Merging one college with another has many consequences that are difficult to see at first. We realized in the summer of 2017 that neither of the two potential partners we had selected offered a bachelor's degree in social work as Wheelock's undergraduate program did. So, I reached out to the field's accreditor—the Council on Social Work Education—to find out what would happen if we went through with a partnership. We were presented with three scenarios, the last of which meant that Wheelock would no longer be an independent institution. This was an idea to which few, if any, members of Wheelock's leadership had adjusted. This is just one of the tricky details we encountered along the way.

Boston University's proposal clearly articulated why Wheelock was important and what Wheelock could offer BU, and vice versa. Of the potential partners, BU had been the most responsive, and President Robert A. Brown had been the most engaged.

David Chard outlined several of the provisions that the two colleges agreed to:

1. BU would invest start-up money in the new Wheelock College of Education and Human Development.
2. BU would offer permanent employment to Wheelock's tenured faculty.
3. Wheelock trustees would be included in the governance of BU Wheelock College.
4. BU would assume all of Wheelock's debt ($37 million), and the new BU Wheelock College would be permitted to keep all or a substantial amount of the Wheelock endowment.
5. BU agreed to "teach out" to degree completion our students in all degrees.
6. BU committed to work diligently to place faculty and staff in positions at BU when possible and to provide some severance and out-placement support for those who could not be accommodated at BU.

With regard to tenure, David explained that tenured faculty at Wheelock could be evaluated for tenure at BU or take modified titles with the same terms of employment as tenured faculty (indefinite permanent employment). Unfortunately, for contingent faculty, including contract and tenure track faculty members, there were no guarantees.

At the end of December 2017, David sent a copy of the draft merger agreement with BU to his remaining vice presidents for input. I told David that I felt we needed to begin referring to Wheelock's closure—using that word—and reiterate to the community that Wheelock College would be closing on May 31, 2018. This was a difficult, but necessary, step.

In October, David had sent his vice presidents a draft of the transition implementation structure, which included more than twenty individual working groups. The structure demonstrated to Wheelock that Boston University was making a tremendous effort to manage the integration at every level of the university. On October 5, the Wheelock board of trustees met for its annual fall meeting. Wheelock's corporation also met that evening for a presentation about the merger, which included a panel with Samantha Fisher, project lead from EY-Parthenon, and Judy Sizer, legal counsel for Wheelock. The panelists focused on the process of how Wheelock had gotten to the point of the merger, together with some agreements already in place (e.g., students would pay Wheelock's rather than BU's tuition rate). After airing concerns about the bachelor of social work teach-out and advocacy for contract faculty, the board voted to authorize President Chard to sign the merger agreement.

By October 11, after many weeks of negotiations, President Chard and President Brown signed the merger agreement. David set up a 9 a.m. conference call with Vice Presidents Jennifer Rice, Cynthia Forrest, Anne Marie Martorana, and me, as well as trustee Chair Sallick to let us know that the merger would be officially announced that day. An email was sent to the Wheelock community informing everyone of this important step in the process. As a footnote to this "point of no return"— the signing of the merger agreement—I'd like to add that it is important not to underestimate the emotional response of every part of a community. While it is essential to consider and respond to faculty, staff, and students, it is also critical to understand that the news of a closure and merger will also cause a wide range of reactions from people not on campus, like alumni, former faculty and staff, and former leadership.

Once the merger was announced, we wanted to move very quickly into making it a reality. First, we communicated with everyone we could imagine: faculty, staff, students, the Massachusetts Department of Elementary and Secondary Education, parents, and reporters covering the story. We reached out to trustees, alumni, donors, former trustees, and all the former Wheelock presidents. We talked to the Colleges of the Fenway and put announcements on Facebook and Twitter. We mailed letters to all alumni with no email address on file.

Later in the month, President Brown met with key members of his merger integration team at BU. His message was that the closure and merger process was going to be difficult for many people who had worked, studied, or been associated with Wheelock College. Consequently, he expected the process to be handled sensitively given the uncertain times. Members of BU's integration team reached out to key contacts listed on the transition documents prepared weeks before. I heard from several senior BU leaders that same day, as did other members of Wheelock's senior leadership team. President Brown had instructed his team to treat Wheelock staff as if they were already part of the Boston University family.

Although there were many uncertainties and emotional responses to the announcement, we realized that over the past few years Wheelock families had grown increasingly worried about the college's financial stability and many were relieved to learn that the Wheelock leadership had prioritized taking care of the students. At the same time, everyone was concerned about finding a way to keep the intimate feeling of a small community like Wheelock in a large, well-resourced institution like Boston University—hoping to achieve what they considered to be the "best of both worlds."

The weightiness and difficulty of leadership during times of crisis cannot be overstated. At this point in time, we and other leaders on campus—whether in official or unofficial leadership positions—became intensely aware of our responsibility to move members of the Wheelock community into a more positive atmosphere about change. The first step was to validate emotional responses to the pending merger and closure. This meant listening more than responding. It can be challenging for leaders to sit quietly, and to listen attentively, but it is a necessary effort during a big transition.

On January 27, 2018, BU hosted Wheelock students and their families at the much-anticipated BU Transition Information and Welcome Day. The event was designed to demonstrate BU's excitement for the merger and to give students and their families a better sense of the university's programs, services, and facilities. The day began with a marching band, red carpet, and greetings from top leadership across the campus. Students then met with academic leaders from schools and colleges where they might pursue their academic programs. The day seemed simultaneously exhilarating, confusing, and frustrating to students and their families. Despite BU's efforts to make this a warm welcome and to allay as many concerns as possible, some students and their parents appeared to feel more anxiety about the transition.

On March 15, 2018, BU's human resources team arrived at Wheelock. They spread out into thirteen offices and began a long day of meetings with Wheelock staff and faculty. For some, the team had offer letters for their new positions at BU. For others, they explained severance packages. So much of our focus for months had been on the people who would not have jobs at BU that we did not anticipate the reaction of those receiving offers, who felt both grateful and anxious. The changes were far from over. We were moving from a year of transition at Wheelock to another at Boston University.

During the process of integrating two institutions, leaders can plan joint programming to communicate to both communities that there will be "life after the merger," in a place where shared interests will thrive. Although students should be the highest priority in merger planning, it is necessary to create opportunities for post-merger careers in support of staff and faculty. Positions may be open in the institution into which one will be merged, and other higher education institutions or other organizations may have availability. It may help to host career days on campus before the merger agreement is fully executed to give faculty and staff the opportunity to pursue other employment options.

Finally, invest in emotions. The closure of an institution is very personal to all involved, and it is important to give people opportunities to adjust to the transition, prepare themselves for the future, and discuss the closure with their colleagues and friends. Time dedicated to lunches, coffees, and celebrations support those who are moving on to the next chapter in their careers. Find a way to honor the hard work and personal investment people have made to your institution. Wheelock chose to do this through an event focused on individuals' unique talents. Events like this offer a pause in the challenges of closure and the anxiety of diminished status while reminding the community of why the institution is special. Emphasize to the governing board members the importance of their selfless actions. Individuals become strong board members because they care about the mission of an institution. The very last thing they can imagine is voting to close it. Leaders need to guide their boards in focus and on positive outcomes. Some mergers fail late in the process owing to trustees who are unable to see their institution without their own participation.

Find a very special way to honor the closing of your institution. This may include an event, a book of memories, or a commemorative pin or print. The memories advanced alongside commemorative items will have an enduring impact on the community and will be a symbol of an acceptance of closure. After closure, members of the community may still look to former leaders to sustain the memories. It is important to be as responsive as possible and to acknowledge those who seek this validation while one focuses on the future: new partnerships, a new position, or perhaps a complete change in career.

As much as we tried, not everyone was happy with our decisions. We were unable to ensure that everyone felt comfortable with the merger. We learned that it helps a great deal to overcommunicate about transitions, to find ways to include alumni, former college leaders, trustees, and former presidents. The process requires patience, and time heals all wounds.

After more than four years post-merger, I am often asked, "How's it going?" In the time that I have started referring to as late-COVID, things at BU Wheelock are looking pretty good. Strangely, the disruption of the merger prepared the legacy BU School of Education and the legacy Wheelock teams for the disruption of the pandemic. We had worked together across two campuses and two legacy groups of faculty, staff, students, alumni, and academic programs to build BU's newest college—Wheelock College of Education and Human Development at BU. Much of the early work of building this new college had taken place on Zoom during the 2018–19 academic year, so we were already Zoom-literate in March 2020 when COVID-19 hit our campus.

At the time, we remarked that we had already been through a closure and merger and that we could also survive the pandemic. We have brought together two historic academic units to build this new college. We have worked together to create new academic departments, new centers and institutes, and new academic programs. We have hired new faculty and staff and built a new strategic plan. We have recommitted ourselves to Boston Public Schools and the city of Boston and pride ourselves on being embedded within our partner schools, hospitals, and nonprofits. Our new mission—transforming the systems that impact learning and human development for a thriving, sustainable, and just future in Boston and beyond—builds on the legacy of Wheelock College's mission to improve the lives of children and families.

References

American Council on Education. n.d. *Chief Academic Officer Survey: THE CAO Job.* https://www.acenet.edu/Documents/Chief-Academic-Officer-Survey-the-CAO-Job.pdf. Accessed June 27, 2020.

Azziz, Ricardo, Guilbert C. Hentschke, Lloyd A. Jacobs, and Bonita C. Jacobs. 2019. *Strategic Mergers in Higher Education.* Baltimore: Johns Hopkins University Press.

Chronicle of Higher Education. 2019. "Which Colleges Have the Largest Endowments?" January 31. https://www.chronicle.com/article/which-colleges-have-the-largest-endowments/.

Churchill, Mary L., and David J. Chard. 2018. *When Colleges Close: Leading in a Time of Crisis.* Baltimore: Johns Hopkins University Press.

EY-Parthenon. 2016. *Strength in Numbers: Strategies for Collaborating in a New Era for Higher Education.* Ernst and Young.

Grawe, Nathan. 2018. *Demographics and the Demand for Higher Education.* Baltimore: Johns Hopkins University Press.

Jaschik, Scott, and Doug Lederman, eds. 2019. *2019 Survey of College and University Chief Academic Officers: A Study by Inside Higher Ed and Gallup*. Washington, DC: Inside Higher Ed; Gallup.

Krantz, Laura. 2015. "Wheelock College Report Finds Financial, Faculty Woes." Boston Globe, June 15. https://www.bostonglobe.com/metro/2015/06/15/wheelock-college-faces-myriad-challenges-report-says/EirQp5Gxx9XCFHKFO8Lz6L/story.html

Martin, James, and James E. Samuels & Associates. 2017. *Consolidating Colleges and Merging Universities: New Strategies for Higher Education Leaders*. Baltimore: Johns Hopkins University Press.

Walumbwa, Fred O., John J. Lawler, and Bruce J. Avolio. 2007. "Leadership, Individual Differences, and Work-Related Attitudes: A Cross-Culture Investigation." *Applied Psychology: An International Review* 56, no. 2: 212–230.

CHAPTER TWO

Rebirth of a University
Martin Methodist College Becomes
the University of Tennessee Southern

MARK LA BRANCHE
President, Martin Methodist College
Chancellor Emeritus, University of Tennessee Southern

WHEN I SAT DOWN for a cup of coffee with the president of the University of Tennessee system, Randy Boyd, in May 2020, neither of us could anticipate what would transpire. Over the next year, with a compelling idea and purposeful strategy, the two institutions experienced a renewed mission and vision. On July 1, 2021, Martin Methodist College spent its first day as the University of Tennessee Southern. This is the story of the merger and what the leadership at what is now UT Southern learned in the process.

In March 2020, President Boyd had just been appointed to a five-year term as president of the University of Tennessee system after having served in an interim capacity for eighteen months. Boyd was an unusual choice to be leader of a state flagship system. A serial entrepreneur, he built a national and international pet supply company that distributed more than four thousand products under brand names Invisible Fence, PetSafe, ScoopFree, and SportDOG. While serving under former Tennessee governor Bill Haslam as special advisor on higher education, Mr. Boyd, an alum of the University of Tennessee–Knoxville, was the architect for Tennessee Promise and Drive to 55 and was the founder and chairman of Tennessee Achieves—all initiatives aimed at increasing the number of Tennesseans with postsecondary degrees to 55% by

2025 and decreasing financial hardship for Tennesseans pursuing degrees. Among Boyd's goals as a new president was to find ways to increasingly fulfill the land grant mission of the system for the benefit of the people of the state of Tennessee. For him this meant providing a higher education pathway for every individual, and that the University of Tennessee would gain reputation not by who it declined but by who it accepted and helped become successful.

On May 29, 2020, President Boyd was completing one of the ninety-five visits he was determined to make to each UT Extension office in Tennessee. While in Giles County, home to Martin Methodist College, President Boyd reached out to me to learn more about Martin Methodist College and its mission in southern Middle Tennessee. I was just completing my third year as president and was working strategically with Martin Methodist staff and trustees to help create a sustainable future for the college. I shared that Martin Methodist College was established in 1870 to provide access to education for women and carried the identity Martin Female College. Now, 150 years later, Martin Methodist College's mission extended to all as a coeducational institution enrolling nine hundred students. Martin Methodist was, and continued to be, primarily a professional and pre-professional school with a liberal arts core, preparing students for occupations in nursing, business, accounting, K–12 education, criminal justice, and social services as well as graduate school.

At the time of our coffee conversation, the administration, staff, and faculty of both institutions were already facing the existential challenges of a worldwide pandemic. At Martin Methodist, a committee of trustees and administration had formed a crisis stability team to address the probable financial ramifications of decreased enrollment and empty residence halls. Prior to the pandemic, the board of trustees had a clear view of our finances and were cognizant of the mounting trends and fierce headwinds in higher education. This required transparency on the part of the administration. While we were managing to end the year in the black, the truth is we were dealing with a significant structural deficit. Our budget was built on unrealistic goals for unrestricted gifts to buoy the annual operating budget and infusions

of unrestricted dollars from estates. We had an unsustainable endowment spending policy of 5.5%. Our tuition discount rate had reached
over 60%. Our staff and faculty averaged .86% in COLA salary increases
over ten years. Building a balanced budget by diminishing the spending power of your employees is not sustainable long term. On a positive note, the college had managed to keep its debt relatively low and
benefited from terms of a USDA loan available to rural institutions. It
also had a discipline of addressing deferred maintenance year by year.

The pandemic brought a whole new sense of urgency around the
long-term sustainability of our mission as an institution. It was determined that along with any short-term measures to ensure viability, we
needed a long-term strategy that included the prospect of partnerships,
collaborations, and mergers. Through the discussions of the crisis stability team, we began to take a broader view through the lens of this
crisis. We increased our efforts to work with colleagues to find ways to
collaborate and increase efficiencies through consortia relationships.
While there was an economy to be won in these kinds of associations,
it was apparent that the impact would not be a major strategy for sustainability. We did not actively pursue a merger, but the idea of it became
less foreign and more palatable. We began to see a horizon of new possibilities. In hushed but hopeful tones, we began to allow ourselves to
speak the word *merger* out loud.

All of these conversations and the current climate meant that when
President Boyd came to call, we were primed for the opportunity. Over
a cup of coffee, President Boyd heard Martin Methodist College's mission, its critical importance to the community, and its challenge of sustainability. Over the course of the conversation, it became apparent
that one way to preserve, enhance, and expand the mission of Martin
Methodist, a mission he shared as the president of a land grant institution, was to go beyond partnerships and combine our efforts through a
merger. In his book, *The Infinite Game*, Simon Sinek states that we must
think about innovation beyond "thinking out of the box." We should be
working under the assumption that there is no "box" at all.[1] Both President Boyd and I subscribed to Sinek's strategy of innovation. One of
the obstacles to "merger" thinking is in seeing a merger as a failure, or

giving up the struggle that our institutions somehow win year in and year out. If we employ "mission" thinking, then an opportunity to preserve, enhance, and expand the mission becomes a huge win.

An Idea Whose Time Had Come

Victor Hugo is quoted as saying, "Nothing else in the world . . . not all the armies . . . is so powerful as an idea whose time has come."[2] Prior to the merger, Southern Middle Tennessee had no public university. Any one of four universities in North Alabama was in closer proximity to its citizens than one in our state. A significant number of students were crossing the border from Southern Middle Tennessee to attend North Alabama universities. With degrees completed in Alabama, they generally did not return to their communities in rural Tennessee, creating a "brain drain."

Martin Methodist College (UT Southern) sits in the middle of what would otherwise have been a higher education desert, with no public university from Chattanooga to Memphis and from the state's southern border to Murfreesboro. While Martin Methodist had filled this gap for well over a century, it was not as affordable as public options and the institution did not have the capacity and resources to fully meet the needs of the region. With Martin Methodist College's stability and sustainability at risk, the region was also at risk of losing access to its only bachelor's- and master's-level institution of higher learning. The acquisition of Martin Methodist by the University of Tennessee system as their fourth undergraduate campus was an idea whose time had come. The mission of providing an accessible and affordable higher education for the purpose of preparing rural students, in a rural setting, for the professions that the region so desperately needed to fill, was compelling. Being able to preserve, enhance, and expand that mission was imperative.

Timing and Process

The process itself would go through a number of stages. It was important to keep the momentum of the process going through each stage.

The merger process began as pre-merger discussion, followed by a commitment to enter the process of merger, then the process of due diligence and merger, and finally an active post-merger period. Merging two institutions is not anything like flipping a light switch. It is akin to peeling an onion. The process peels back one layer after another only to reveal seemingly unending levels of detail. We discovered that our stakeholders had varying levels of tolerance for the pace of change. Both President Boyd and I admitted to our boards that this was going to be uncomfortable in a number of ways. One was definitely the pace by which we needed to proceed.

Our fiscal years coincided, each beginning July 1. We agreed that a target date for the merger could be the beginning of our next fiscal year, July 1, 2021. Then together, we determined what had to be completed to facilitate the successful acquisition on July 1, 2021. The University of Tennessee assigned a project manager to coordinate our steps and calendar of critical deadlines. Our teams framed the merger process around the required authorizations and approvals that we needed. We knew that we would have to align our process with the Southern Association of Colleges and Schools (SACSCOC) calendar of accreditation, which required us to give a six-month notification of a potential change of ownership. We also knew that the University of Tennessee would need approval and budgetary consideration from the Tennessee General Assembly, and Martin Methodist College would need approval from the Tennessee Conference of the United Methodist Church. Working backward from the date we hoped to merge, we were able to create a timeline based on these requirements.

December 2020—Notify SACSCOC of potential change of ownership.
January 2021—Tennessee General Assembly begins legislative session.
February 2021—Governor Bill Lee puts forward the state budget.
March 2021—Prepare and submit prospectus to SACSCOC.
June 2021—Seek SACSCOC board approval for merger within thirty days.

June 2021—Tennessee Conference of the United Methodist Church meets.

July 2021—Martin Methodist College becomes UT Southern.

Quiet but Diligent Research

Once the timeline was set, the next critical step became depositing the idea among stakeholders and receiving feedback. This was a quiet phase. In this stage, it was important that both institutions committed to confidentiality by signing a nondisclosure agreement as we tested the idea among the primary decision makers and essential constituencies. The University of Tennessee system is made up of nine campuses all governed by one board with eleven members. As an institution of the state, public meeting laws prohibited the board from deliberating in private. Therefore, in order to comply with the law, board members needed to be approached individually to collect their general impressions, thoughts, questions, and concerns. The Martin Methodist Board of Trustees was not subject to the same public meeting laws. The discussion began with the chairman of the board of trustees. Individual trustees were then engaged by the board chair and myself to collect their general impressions along with their thoughts, questions, and concerns.

Initial confidential conversations were also held with local elected leaders, college and university administrators, alumni leadership, and church leadership. While the idea was generally received with enthusiasm in each conversation, we were also able to collect some of the questions and concerns that would definitely need to be addressed as we entered into a more public phase.

During this time, the University of Tennessee System also entered into a round of initial due diligence that included a cursory evaluation of our physical plant and financial position, and the preliminary report was favorable. A more thorough examination of these areas and an in-depth feasibility study would take place later in the process. They also reviewed our accreditation standing and learned that Martin Methodist College had recently completed its ten-year reaffirmation with no recommendations or further reports required.

Then the Martin Methodist board and MMC administration gathered to discuss the opportunity face-to-face with the UT system administration, to hear from them, share our enthusiasm and concerns, and to ask questions. The gathering began, as any good negotiation does, with identifying the nonnegotiables. For Martin Methodist trustees, preserving the mission they had stewarded for the past century and a half was nonnegotiable. The board had to be convinced that the role of MMC as a college of opportunity for first-generation and Pell-eligible rural students would not only continue but benefit from the merger.

Going Public and Building Trust

As we continued our conversations, it was generally acknowledged that there was a limit to our ability to keep the idea quiet and confidential. It would be important that we move into a more public phase rather quickly so that the two institutions could remain in control of the narrative. With a strong positive response and a list of questions and concerns from stakeholders, it was time to publicly express the intent of both institutions to begin the process of merging. On September 11, 2020, both boards approved a letter of intent, accompanied by a nondisclosure agreement and an initial terms of agreement sheet outlining a broad framework of expectations, requirements, and contingencies. The terms of the merger would become more and more defined as the process moved through its stages. Both boards took comfort that the terms included an exit clause that would allow either party to back out at any time before the actual acquisition agreement was signed.

While the exit clause was certainly a prudent thing to include, it put Martin Methodist College in an ambiguous and vulnerable position. MMC incurred a significant amount of vulnerability by going public. In the event of a failure to merge, the University of Tennessee would continue as before. Martin Methodist College had more to lose and would certainly be left in a weaker position reputationally.

Stephen M. R. Covey reveals in his book *The Speed of Trust* that "the simple, often overlooked fact is this: work gets done with and through people. There's nothing more impactful on people, their work, and their performance, than trust."[3] A certain level of trust would be absolutely essential to our work. And with trust, a certain willingness to be vulnerable and uncomfortable.

Having adequate legal guidance and representation was an important part of building trust between the two institutions and between the institutions and the community. While the University of Tennessee system already employed a team of attorneys, Martin Methodist had a retainer contract that only allowed for a limited scope of advice and legal counsel. The MMC board and administration set out to find an experienced law firm to represent us that would have the combined expertise to address the complexities of the merger. We chose a firm that had broad experience in higher education, acquisitions and mergers, real estate, endowments, and charitable foundations.

It quickly became apparent that this merger was a novel event, and that what we were attempting together would be breaking new ground. While neither institution's attorneys had the benefit of precedent, they did know what questions needed to be answered and what issues needed to be addressed. Everyone benefited from the work the attorneys did clarifying the expectations of the schools as we were coming from two different organizational cultures, private and public. The attorneys were also invaluable in the preparation of the many required documents, as the difficult application process involved in moving a nonprofit corporation into state hands required the approval of the attorney general of the state of Tennessee.

Dedication and Diligence

Once both the UT system and Martin Methodist College signed the letter of intent, both groups began a more in-depth process of due diligence. UT began a comprehensive assessment of our physical plant and prepared a five-year projection of required capital maintenance. They conducted a deeper look into the finances and operations of the college and completed a feasibility study. Simultaneously, Martin Methodist College trustees did their due diligence by compiling several surveys of its various stakeholders that would be used to inform our priorities, expectations, and terms of agreement. This work led to the terms including the expectation that the jobs of Martin Methodist employees would be secure in the acquisition and that tenured faculty would keep their tenure status with the approval of the UT system board. It was also demonstrated that employee benefits would be enhanced through becoming state employees. A transition to becoming state of Tennessee employees would mean significantly lower insurance costs and a higher pension match for MMC employees. The Martin board of trustees also asked to retain the college's endowment in what would become the Martin Methodist College Charitable Foundation for the benefit of the University of Tennessee Southern. The forming of the charitable foundation felt like a tangible way to help guard the historic mission of the college and the spirit and purpose for which funds were given. The foundation would steward the resources but not engage in future fundraising. This was agreeable to both parties. All of this was presented to the trustees of MMC and UT in December 2021 as the basis for a further resolution approving the pursuit of all necessary authorizations and approvals to complete the acquisition.

The Tennessee General Assembly would ultimately have to approve the recurring and nonrecurring resources to establish the new university campus. In preparation for the legislative session that began in January 2021, work started immediately to communicate the importance and benefit of the merger to our elected officials. President Randy Boyd and I visited leaders in each of the thirteen counties of Southern Middle Tennessee to share the opportunity, answer questions, and encourage each town and each county to present resolutions to the governor and legislature in support of the acquisition. Resolutions were prepared and presented by every town and county we visited. In addition to these resolutions, we gathered personal letters of support from community and business leaders across the region.

Mission Communication

While there were many technical aspects to consider in the process of our merger with UT, the most critical ingredients for success were social. Managing our communications through a comprehensive plan was key to addressing the social elements of the process.

Our public communications began with the announcement of our intent to merge. On the same day, we launched a microsite, linked to the front page of our main website, that we had prepared to use for all forms of communication about the merger. The MMC to UT website served as both a source of new updates and an archive of previous communications including announcements, press releases, and an extensive FAQ list. The microsite served as a centralized source of well-vetted information and helped to reduce misinformation and rumor throughout the merger process.

The University of Tennessee system and Martin Methodist College worked to clearly communicate our compelling story. We told the story we were writing together, of two universities who were seizing the opportunity to place mission over identity. Our teams at Martin Methodist wanted to be sure the narrative clearly presented that the opportunity before us was not born out of necessity but was a way to secure and expand the mission we so greatly valued. We were not experiencing untenable financial circumstances and the college had relative stability. We were not looking for a savior, but a partner. In fact, it was our strengths rather than our weaknesses that made our institution an attractive partner for the University of Tennessee.

As we created a communication plan, we intentionally built in space for empathy and compassion. It was important for us to be clear with everyone involved that we were entering into a season where things would sometimes feel ambiguous or uncertain. I assured our teams and stakeholders that I would share all I could, when I could, but there were going to be some questions that did not yet have answers. It was helpful for me and others in leadership to ask people simply and with genuine curiosity, "What is making you feel anxious?" In most cases we were able to work together to help relieve that anxiety.

As details continued to fall into place, we entered into a period of waiting that I referred to as a liminal season. In "Merger Musings," one of the regular epistles I would send to our learning community, I borrowed from my favorite contemporary theologian, Richard Rohr, where he speaks to the majesty and mystery of what he calls this "sacred space" of liminality: ". . . where we are betwixt and between the familiar and the completely unknown. There alone is our old world left behind, while we are not yet sure of the new existence. That's a good space where genuine newness can begin. Get there often and stay as long as you can by whatever means possible. . . . This is the sacred space where the old world is able to fall apart, and a bigger world is revealed."[4]

These regular Merger Musings revealed the empathy of the administration and let colleagues know that their feelings of anxiety or unease were valid, even expected. Through these epistles we showed them, and reminded ourselves, that they were not alone, that we were all in this together.

Resistance

No big change occurs without some resistance. Resistance to the merger came in a number of forms, including social media comments and emails, news articles, and private conversations. Soon after the letter of intent became public, resistance came in the form of a press article arguing against the necessity of such an acquisition and its cost to the state.

We knew that institutions already operating within the state system would have concerns about how adding another campus might affect them. One university publicly called the move into question and began to lobby against the acquisition. However, the idea had garnered such strong and enthusiastic support from strategic leaders during the quiet phase of our process that when the intent became public, as one person remarked, "the train was already a long way down the tracks." Rather than continue in opposition, the university requested certain covenants from the UT system that would limit our geographical facility to exclude their immediate counties and a covenant not to oppose the university's future attempts to add specific programs.

Resistance also came from a small number of alumni who expressed their strong opposition to the merger, but they were not able to garner a significant following. The alumni concerns were valid and related to both real and perceived losses—the losses of tradition, identity, and church-relatedness. As leaders at Martin Methodist College, we could empathize with them. The truth was, a majority of our learning community saw this as a bittersweet development. We all had mixed feelings. Any great transformation comes with the excitement of opportunity and the grief of loss.

Church Relationship Matters

Martin Methodist College is a church-related institution. For United Methodists, gaining knowledge has always been a divine pursuit and the church feels a social responsibility to ensure that education is available to all. Martin Methodist College began in the basement of Pulaski First United Methodist Church in order to make the opportunity for an education available to women. Over the past 150 years, the college has expanded this mission beyond what its founders imagined. With this merger, we would have an unprecedented opportunity to expand the mission exponentially. The leaders of the Tennessee Conference of the United Methodist Church were friendly to the idea but had questions regarding what becoming a secular institution would mean to spiritual life on campus and what would become of a number of faith-based initiatives that had begun as a part of MMC.

A legal matter that needed to be addressed early in the merger negotiation process was the matter of the United Methodist Church's "trust clause." The "trust clause" is clear in the case of church ownership. The trustees of a United Methodist conference control the ownership of each church building and property of United Methodist churches within its conference. The clause is less clear when it comes to institutions related to the church, such as colleges and universities. Not wanting to test the legalities of ownership, the board of trustees of Martin Methodist College sought a waiver of the "trust clause" by the trustees of the Tennessee Conference of the United Methodist Church, allowing the acquisition to go forward.

The Tennessee Conference trustees negotiated a resolution to waive the "trust clause." This resolution contained several expectations and agreements that would ultimately respond to their concerns. First, the resolution included retaining the current Martin Methodist endowment in a charitable foundation to ensure that the purpose of each account was fulfilled. The conference trustees believed that the endowment was established and had grown primarily through the generosity of United Methodist churches and congregants. As stated earlier, the Martin Methodist College trustees also wanted to retain the endowment as a tangible way to express the guarding of the college's mission. Approximately 20% of the endowment was designated to support United Methodist students and 20% supported the Turner Center for Rural Vitality, where initiatives were in partnership with the rural faith community. Finally, the church wanted to ensure that the United Methodist ministry to students would continue. The administration worked with the United Methodist Higher Education Foundation to repurpose an endowment fund held to benefit MMC student scholarships for use in the establishment and sustainment of a Wesley student ministry. In December 2020, the conference trustees passed the resolution waiving the "trust clause," preparing the way for its approval by the Tennessee Annual Conference delegates in June 2021.

Money, Money, Money

As a part of the preparation for merger, the UT system commissioned the Huron Higher Education Consulting Group to do a feasibility study. The study predicted a conservative level of institutional growth and projected three years of revenue. The study indicated that once becoming part of the UT System, MMC would experience a loss of approximately $350,000 in the first year based on level growth, and also that Martin Methodist College would enter into the agreement at least one million dollars into its line of credit on July 1, 2021. This presented a liability to UT that had not been previously contemplated. It is also the case that institutions within the UT system do not have access to lines of credit. While the study predicted that growth would lead to a healthy surplus within three years, there were no guarantees. We knew these liabilities could raise concern among legislators and become a talking point for those who would resist.

In January 2021, President Boyd challenged Martin Methodist to raise one million dollars in gifts to match a $1 million pledge by the Boyd Family Foundation. This would ensure a strong financial footing and obviate challenges from legislators and other parties based on finances. The advancement team at Martin Methodist College enthusiastically accepted the challenge and immediately began to identify, cultivate, and solicit donors. The team identified more than fifty prospects that included individuals, foundations, corporations, and government entities. With the power of this compelling idea and prospective opportunity, President Boyd and I began a series of visits, which along with the efforts of our advancement team garnered unprecedented support. A total of three million dollars was raised ahead of the acquisition. In addition to this successful fundraising, several tranches of CARES Act money, decreased expenses as a result of COVID-19 restrictions on travel, and a deliberate and disciplined approach to spending led to MMC being in a significantly different financial position on July 1 than Huron projected. When the financial projections were brought to the boards for their final vote on June 25, 2021, Martin Methodist would end their fiscal year without a line of credit balance and the new university would now project a surplus of 4.5 million in its first year with level enrollment.

Counting the Cost

The process of merger and acquisition is expensive if done well. Both institutions needed to dedicate many, many hours of staff time to this effort. The UT system bought its staff of lawyers, administrators, governmental affairs professionals, and marketing, communication, and public relations experts to the effort. Beyond this, the UT System enlisted the support of outside consulting groups. Having a much smaller staff, Martin Methodist needed to augment its team by contracting with additional third parties such as a law firm and a public relations consultant group. Approximately $250,000 dollars would be spent on branding our new university. Our institutional and athletic brand needed to change, and we wanted to have as much of the campus branded as possible on day one. In order to immediately benefit from our new identity and brand, we launched several flights of targeted and themed social media at a cost of more than $100,000. To address these costs, the UT system asked for and received $1 million to offset start-up costs for the new university from the state. This was in addition to the 5.1 million in recurring funding that would allow us to drop our tuition sticker price by 60%.

A Growing Presumption

As each authorization was secured, and as enthusiasm and support grew, the presumption of a successful merger also grew. Both institutions needed to carefully balance anticipatory preparation with the importance of not getting out ahead of decision makers. There was an opportunity to leverage the momentum and presumptive change in our efforts to retain and enroll students in the fall of 2021, and by the time the merger became official on July 1, we would be very late in the recruitment cycle. Together we could start to promote the prospective change as long as we were clear that the merger still required a number of pending approvals. Our financial aid office began to distribute aid packages to our current and prospective students using what would be the new cost of attendance and financial aid estimates, though they were still pending the necessary approvals for the merger.

Memorializing the Past and Preparing for the Future

After the governor included recurring and nonrecurring funding in his budget released in early February 2021, the UT system began transition planning in earnest. Once the budget passed the legislature in April 2021, the UT system began to implement all the necessary steps for a clean acquisition on July 1. We immediately began to align our business practices and prepare our employees for transition to state higher education employees. There would be certifications of résumés, background checks, and numerous details regarding access to employee benefits that needed to be completed.

The branding process also began in earnest. This was an opportunity to create buy-in for the campus and community. Numerous surveys revealed that there were two elements of MMC branding that all constituents saw as most reflective of our identity and wanted to bring forward in some way as the new brand for our university was created. The first was the iconic columns that stand tall on our historic green, providing a stage and focal point for convocations, graduations, and concerts. Second, it was important to our entire community to include the primary color of MMC, red, in some way. We were able to preserve red as a secondary color in our athletic branding. Where we were once Redhawks, we became Firehawks using both UT orange and MMC red. A committee that included the faculty senate, faculty council, and student government association was tasked with the design of a new university seal, which was a wonderful way to preserve the element of the columns. Post-merger, the columns also found a place in the logo of our Alumni Society, linking the past tradition with our new identity.

The institution would need a new name. Historically, the universities in the Tennessee system took on the name of the city where they are located: UT Knoxville, UT Martin, UT Chattanooga. In our case it was paramount that the institution be identified with not just our city, but with our region in order to create an immediate sense of ownership across Southern Middle Tennessee. While UT Pulaski garnered a fair amount of support in the final preference survey, primarily from local community members, the University of Tennessee Southern came out on top.

In the months leading up to the merger, Martin Methodist administration and trustees focused on ways to memorialize the 151-year mission and tradition of the college. This was accomplished in the recognition and naming of a number of programs and places on campus to memorialize the important figures in Martin Methodist history. The Martin name was kept as the name of our School of Liberal Arts.

It was also important to be deliberate about appropriately marking the turning points. After the church voted its final approval in June, the college held a worship service led by our chaplain, with our bishop participating. The pastor of Pulaski First United Methodist Church, an MMC alum, brought the message. We called it a "Celebration of Thanksgiving and Remembrance."

Recognizing that there was no small amount of grief in letting go of the past, we arranged a staff and faculty lunch on the green and invited former staff, faculty, and faculty emeriti to attend. Long-term employees, faculty, and staff were invited to share reflections, favorite stories, and legends from their time at Martin.

Closing the Deal

On June 25, with all authorizations and approvals received, and with terms of the acquisition settled, both boards voted unanimously to approve the merger and the UT System Board voted to accept President Boyd's recommendation to appoint the last president of Martin Methodist College as the first chancellor of the university.

Signage on the Martin campus began to transition immediately. Plans were already in place for a Merger Eve watch party on the town square and a formal ribbon cutting on the green the next morning, July 1. Tennessee governor Bill Lee and a cast of state leadership joined President Boyd and me in the shadow of the iconic columns to inaugurate the University of Tennessee Southern.

We Are Not in Kansas Anymore

It did not take long to see that we were entering into a new and very different landscape. We witnessed immediate and significant increases in the number of inquiries and applications; the pace of applications increased by more than 120%. Student retention in the spring to fall semester also increased, likely in correlation with our new identity and lower tuition. Our new student enrollment grew by almost 25% in the fall of 2021 over the fall of 2020. As a public university, we also began to experience preferred access to the public high schools. We now have been brought into the family, including bearing the reputation of the University of Tennessee system. This was far and away a tremendously positive development. However, being that the reputation was primarily associated with the flagship Knoxville campus, it could also bring concern regarding commonly held assumptions about UTK. Will we become too selective? Will we become large and impersonal? Will we start fraternities and sororities? Will we actively promote certain lifestyles, and so on? There were those who conflated the wealth of an SEC school with our financial position. I heard on more than one occasion, "You don't need my money." We will continue to need to communicate and promote our own identity as an autonomous campus with a unique mission and culture.

We now find ourselves in a whole new world of governmental constituent affairs. While as a private college we carefully crafted our communications to our constituents, being a public institution under the auspices of the state and general assembly, supported by the taxpayer, requires a much higher level of scrutiny. Official messages need to be passed through various levels and various filters before the public stance of the institution can be communicated. A recent communication, responding to a surge in COVID-19 cases, that urged vaccines and required masking in some cases passed through dozens of hands and numerous revisions before its final release. Legislation supporting freedom of speech reduces our options in responding to speech formerly prohibited on our private campus, including speech we would consider vulgar and immoral.

It was apparent from the very start that we would be less nimble. New programs require an extended process and ultimate approval by the Tennessee Higher Education Commission. Searches for faculty and staff include a system-level process that adds a few steps and requires more time. Future searches will require more anticipation and planning.

While we will be living into this transition for the next few years, becoming assimilated, acclimated, and acculturated, it is already abundantly clear that despite a number of drawbacks, the acquisition promises to serve our mission in Southern Middle Tennessee in calculable and incalculable ways. The number of new students in the first class of UTS students increased by almost 25% over the previous year. With the highest increase in enrollment of any state institution overall, enrollment increased by 7.7% in the fall of 2021. Fall 2022 enrollment continued to climb at UTS, with a 5.2% increase in undergraduate students and a striking 58.3% in graduate students. Fall 2022 also saw a rise in retention of first-time fall freshmen of more than 11%. In its first year the University of Tennessee recorded an all-time high in fundraising and a 300% increase in the number of individual donors over the previous year.

Having served as the thirty-first and last president of Martin Methodist College and the first chancellor of the University of Tennessee, my role was a transitional one. On July 1, 2022, I was appointed as special assistant to the president of the UT system and honored with the title chancellor emeritus. Dr. Linda Martin, VPAA for the UT system, was appointed interim chancellor while the process of preparing for and completing a search for the next chancellor could be completed.

Notes

1. Simon Sinek. 2020. *The Infinite Game* (New York: Penguin).
2. Victor Hugo Quotes. (n.d.). Quotes.net. Retrieved August 17, 2021, from https://www .quotes.net/quote/966.
3. Stephen M. R. Covey and R. R. Merrill. 2018. *The Speed of Trust: The One Thing That Changes Everything* (New York: Free Press).
4. R. Rohr. 1999. *Everything Belongs: The Gift of Contemplative Prayer*. New York: Crossroad Publishing Company.

CHAPTER THREE

Intractable Path to an Alternative Future

Expanding and Filling the Strategic Toolbox

CHRISTINE PLUNKETT

President, Iowa Wesleyan University

ON NOVEMBER 1, 2018, following a somber board meeting, the Iowa Wesleyan University Board of Trustees announced the likely imminent closure of the historic 176-year-old university in rural Southeast Iowa. The announcement followed months of careful analysis and sobering discussion of the university's financial position and future enrollment outlook. It also followed years of continued failing financial responsibility composite scores, ongoing financial monitoring by the Higher Learning Commission, and heightened cash monitoring by the Department of Education.

More than three years after announcing impending closure, not only is Iowa Wesleyan University still operating, but it has made significant strides in efforts to reach financial sustainability through increased enrollment and improved retention rates. Beyond that, the university has taken innovative steps to establish itself as an economic development force in rural Southeast Iowa.

Those three years were marked by efforts to bolster the university's financial position and map a way forward. The efforts included initiatives for increased fundraising, a significant enhancement of student support services, and steps to establish a partnership that could lead to a turnaround in circumstances. A sense of urgency, but not panic, pervaded the process. There was no denying the sobering reality of the circumstances, but "leadership with purpose" characterized those years. There was clearly not a panacea for all the university's challenges, and the goal became one of filling our toolbox with multiple tools for success.

Our turnaround in circumstances, including an unprecedented increase in undergraduate enrollment, has required nimble, courageous, engaged, and forward-looking leadership by the board of trustees and administration. The Iowa Wesleyan University Board of Trustees, while keenly aware of its fiduciary responsibilities, has been willing to take carefully considered risks in the interests of preserving a historic institution and providing expanded educational opportunities to an underserved and under-resourced population of students in a rural corner of the American Midwest.

As we continue to strive toward sustainability, we are well aware of ongoing threats. The higher education landscape continues to change, and the sense of urgency must be maintained. Woven throughout the university's history is a shared sense of duty that has carried us through repeated challenges for nearly two centuries. Above all, our evolution has required an understanding that as the world changes, so too must our mission—the students of today are not the same as the students of yesterday. Our story is one of broadening our perspectives to create an alternative future that not only sustains the university but supports our rural region as well.

A brief history of Iowa Wesleyan will help provide context for the difficult decisions the university has faced over the past several years. Founded in 1842 and affiliated with the United Methodist Church, Iowa Wesleyan University is a fully accredited, coeducational liberal arts university with a current undergraduate enrollment of 700 students and a total head count of 850 students. The university is known for its unusually diverse population of students. The 100-plus international students on campus hail from 35 countries around the world. For several years, Iowa Wesleyan has been ranked as the most ethnically and economically diverse campus in Iowa, and among the six most diverse campuses in the Midwest. In 2018, with Hispanic students making up more than 10% of total enrollment, Iowa Wesleyan became the first higher education institution in Iowa to be affiliated with HACU, the Hispanic Association of Colleges and Universities. The university, which is committed to fostering a student-centered community and providing an accessible and affordable education, is also ranked a top regional college in the Midwest by US News and World Report.

Iowa Wesleyan has a rich history of innovation in education, is a pioneer in the sciences, and is at the forefront of educational opportunities for women. Graduates include Belle Babb Mansfield (1866), who was the first woman admitted to the bar in the United States, becoming the first female lawyer in the country. The university's first Black female graduate was Susan Mosely Grandison (1885), and the first documented international student, Keyroku Miyazaki from Japan, attended from 1890 to 1891. In 1869, seven female Iowa Wesleyan students founded the P.E.O. Sisterhood, a philanthropic organization that provides educational opportunities for female students. The organization now boasts more than 230,000 members in chapters around the world. In 1958, Iowa Wesleyan graduate James Van Allen (1935) discovered the earth's radiation belts that now bear his name. NASA astronaut Peggy Whitson (1981), who set numerous records on three missions between 2002 and 2017, became the first female commander of the International Space Station in 2007.

The academic programs at Iowa Wesleyan include undergraduate, graduate, and online learning. The university has long been a leader in service learning and field experience. Service learning is integrated into the curriculum, ensuring that all students connect classroom learning with service to others, and all students are required to complete an internship as part of their graduation requirements. Many of these internships lead to full-time employment opportunities after graduation.

Located in Mount Pleasant, Iowa, a rural community of about 9,000 residents, Iowa Wesleyan offers a variety of arts and cultural opportunities for Southeast Iowa. Art shows, concerts, lectures, and plays take place throughout the year, and most are open to the public at no charge. The Southeast Iowa Symphony Orchestra is based on campus. The university serves as a regional resource for other organizations, inviting all Iowa nonprofit entities to utilize campus meeting facilities, when available, at no charge. These close ties to our community were crucial when our troubling announcement was made in 2018, as community members came to the table when they were most needed.

The university enjoyed its highest enrollment levels throughout the 1960s, reaching an enrollment of close to 1,000 undergraduates in 1967. Throughout the early 2000s, the university struggled with low retention rates for first-time freshmen, seldom reaching 50%. Concerned that the institution's athletic programs were attracting students who were academically unprepared for college study, the board chose in 2011 to eliminate athletic scholarships by moving from NAIA to NCAA Division III athletics. Over the next several years, undergraduate enrollment dropped precipitously to just 386 students by 2015. At the same time, the university was struggling under the weight of more than $21 million in long-term debt. The outlook for reaching a sustainable level of revenue was increasingly bleak.

Significant strides toward sustainability were made between 2015 and 2018. By the fall of 2018, undergraduate enrollment had increased to 564 and the university had successfully restructured its debt through a USDA Rural Development loan. Nevertheless, retention rates remained low, USDA loan payments were in deferral, and the runway seemed too short to find a way forward.

Following the university's 2018 announcement of impending closure, the community of Mount Pleasant, along with businesses, alumni, and individuals from across the broader region, rallied and raised more than $1 million in transitional funds to provide the university with a brief window of time to consider alternatives to closing. Our community members had provided the runway we needed, but the administration and board recognized there was little time to lose in choosing a new direction.

Fortunately, a 2016 restructuring of the board had prepared the trustees well for the challenging circumstances of decision-making under pressure. Abandoning its traditional committee structure, which was largely focused on operations, the board established three "groups" focused on mission, resources, and governance. Under the new structure, the board learned to conduct its work through generative discussions, with a focus on fiduciary responsibilities and overarching strategic goals. Board meetings now consistently included an introductory key issue topic—typically a presentation by faculty members, students, or outside professionals associated with higher education. These key issue presentations fed directly into the generative model of reflective dialogue and provided trustees with a sense of purpose and mission. The result was a board that was well aligned with the administration. With a better understanding of current issues and potential solutions, trustees became significantly more proactive than reactive.

I joined the administrative team at Iowa Wesleyan in July 2015 through the Registry for College and University Presidents, appointed to an interim chief financial officer role by President Steven Titus. Much of the first year of my appointment was occupied with efforts to restructure the university's significant debt, which consisted of numerous loans through several lenders at varying interest rates. In October 2016, the university closed on two USDA Community Facilities loans: a $5 million USDA-guaranteed loan through a regional bank and a $21 million direct loan through the USDA. The restructured debt, offered with favorable terms and a low interest rate, provided the university with a lengthened timeline and some additional funds for implementing proposed new growth strategies.

During this period, the university undertook numerous growth initiatives. Efforts to improve student retention rates were bolstered through participation in the inaugural cohort of the Higher Learning Commission's Persistence and Completion Academy in 2014. This program led to the formation of Iowa Wesleyan's Persistence and Completion Council, a committee that continues its work today. The group includes members from all areas of university operations and focuses on a wide range of initiatives to better serve our students and ensure their success. By the fall semester of 2017, the retention rate for first-year freshmen had increased to 66%, after a decade during which retention rates averaged 47%. The same year, overall student persistence rates increased to 73%, following ten years with rates averaging 66%.

At the same time, a new partnership with Royall and Company (now EAB) was yielding a reversal in the university's faltering enrollments. After five years of declining undergraduate enrollment, a 23% increase in the fall of 2016 began a growth trend that has continued over the past five years. The addition of six new athletic programs between 2017 and 2021 provided an additional boost to enrollment efforts, with total athletic rosters more than doubling from 217 in the fall of 2017 to 450 in fall 2021.

Despite these clear signs of progress and a more engaged board, the financial picture at the university remained unstable. A going concern analysis made as part of the annual financial audit in the fall of 2018 reflected fundraising shortfalls. Cash projections through the following year, even with substantial faculty and staff cuts under consideration, were insufficient to sustain operations. Exhaustion had led to a sense of futility, and on November 1, 2018, following a special meeting of the board of trustees, President Steven Titus conveyed the seriousness of the situation to the Iowa Wesleyan community: "The university does not have a healthy endowment or extensive donor network. We have attempted to secure funding to establish a solid financial base. Unfortunately, several anticipated gifts simply have not materialized. At this moment, the university does not have the required financial underpinnings to bridge the gap between strong enrollment and new programming, and the money needed to keep the institution open."

He went on to explain that the board would be reconvening in two weeks, on November 15, to consider the future of the university: "Today, the board of trustees voted to reconvene on November 15, 2018, to consider the future of the institution. Therefore, we are actively and aggressively pursuing additional funding sources, and new and innovative partnerships, collaborations, and supporters. The next 14 days are extremely important as we meet with the USDA, regional business and community leaders, and partners in higher education to explore alternatives."

The public announcement of possible closure was a tremendous risk, as well as a wakeup call. We understood the risks—the potential for a catastrophic enrollment decline (which thankfully did not occur) and long-term negative perceptions that would be difficult to overcome. The wakeup call served its purpose. The board and community rallied, fully understanding that wishful thinking was not enough and that concrete plans to pursue new alternatives were necessary.

Just days later, President Titus and I arrived for the first day of the annual Registry for College and University Presidents Symposium in Saint Augustine, Florida, along with our provost, Dr. DeWayne Frazier. On the morning of November 7, the three of us gathered with several of the executive officers of the registry and its consulting branch, Registry Advisory Services (RAS), to discuss Iowa Wesleyan's circumstances and to consider the future. Following a conference call with Iowa Wesleyan's board leadership, a decision was made to immediately launch an Alternative Futures initiative to identify a new direction that could forestall closure of the university.

The following day, Dr. Frazier and I, along with two of my Registry colleagues from other institutions, were giving a presentation on the importance of higher education administrators working "across the aisle" with one another. The presentation pointed out the ways in which demographic trends and shifting enrollment patterns threaten revenue streams, and the importance of creative and flexible leadership and nimble boards in preparing for the future. While no public mention was made of Iowa Wesleyan's dire circumstances back in Mount Pleasant, one of the closing slides in our presentation stated: "Even through applying these strategies, fragile institutions may not be able to successfully navigate the headwinds."

While we were feeling somewhat more optimistic about the Alternative Futures approach, I'm not sure our audience fully recognized the real weight of that statement on Dr. Frazier and me that day.

Behind the scenes, a full-court fundraising effort was underway to secure the funds needed to continue operations through our Alternative Futures transition period. A letter received by board chair Annette

Scieszinski on November 14 from the executive vice president of the Mount Pleasant Area Chamber Alliance summed up the importance of Iowa Wesleyan to the region:

> We have come to rely on Iowa Wesleyan University as a driving force of our economy. Not only for the educational aspect but also for the important service learning that is integrated into the curriculum which has helped so many projects around our community.
>
> We rely on Iowa Wesleyan for a variety of arts and cultural opportunities for Southeast Iowa. The Southeast Iowa Symphony, the art shows, concerts, lectures, and plays that take place throughout the year are enjoyed not only by the students but by our residents as well. Likewise, the University's involvement in the NCAA athletic program is a source of entertainment and pride for many community members.
>
> Iowa Wesleyan University's economic impact of $55.1 million is vital to our economy and more than 150 jobs affiliated with Iowa Wesleyan are crucial to our well-being. Therefore, we are asking you to continue operations through May 2019 and pursue a new, alternative, and sustainable future for the University.

On November 15, 2018, the board reconvened to review new information and reach a final decision on the university's future. In addition to the university's trustees and senior administrative team, the meeting's participants included university legal counsel, a senior registry consultant, and a communications advisor.

The president's report to the board at that meeting indicated that $1.4 million had been raised since the November 1 announcement of possible closure, providing much of the necessary cash to carry the university through a necessarily brief transition period while seeking a partner. The Rev. Dr. Bill Nelson from RAS outlined the "alternative futures" process, which would include preparing a request for proposals, reviewing all submitted proposals for strength and fit, choosing finalists, and completing due diligence in the selection of a final partner. Final actions taken by the board during that meeting included:

- That the university continue operations through and beyond May 2019.
- That an Alternative Futures Project be adopted and implemented to secure partnership for a sustainable future for the university, the local community, and the region.
- That a New Directions Team be authorized and established, made up of members of the Iowa Wesleyan Board of Trustees and administration.
- That Registry Advisory Services be retained to assist with the implementation of a timely and efficient process for securing partnership.

That afternoon, President Titus communicated the meeting's outcome to the IW faculty, staff, and students:

Iowa Wesleyan University's Board of Trustees voted to move forward, continuing operations at the university after required funding was secured through support from alumni, friends and community and collaboration with the USDA Rural Development.

We are very happy to continue the mission of Iowa Wesleyan, which is to educate the next generation of leaders and be an economic engine for Southeast Iowa.

The Board will be actively pursuing new partnerships to create a more sustainable future for the university, community and region. A New Directions Team has been established to lead this effort.

An aggressive timeline was established and followed during the ensuing months. The first meeting of the newly appointed New Directions Team (NDT), headed by the chair of the board's Resource Group, Robert Miller, and consisting of seven trustees and President Titus, as well as several ex-officio administrators, was held on December 6. During that meeting, a draft RFP was reviewed, and a preliminary information packet about the university was presented and discussed. On December 7, a final draft of the RFP was distributed for further comment, and a final version was approved by the chair of the NDT and the president on December 10. RFPs were distributed to 242 higher education institutions across the country that same week.

On January 9, 2019, the university hosted a "town hall" meeting for a diverse group of attendees: trustees, faculty, staff, community members, business owners, local and regional leaders, and alumni. During that meeting, it was announced that 27 expressions of interest were received in response to the RFP. On February 8, the New Directions Team met and reviewed 10 proposals that were deemed to be of the most interest. That meeting resulted in a recommendation that four of the proposals be advanced to an interview stage. One institution withdrew in the ensuing days, leaving three viable proposals. By mid-February, campus visits from all three contenders were scheduled, and by the first week of March, a letter of intent and nondisclosure agreement had been signed with Florida's Saint Leo University, and an intensive due diligence process was launched.

Throughout the first two months of due diligence, confidentiality was maintained, and no public disclosure was made of our selected partner. On April 30, President Titus announced to the Iowa Wesleyan community that Saint Leo University was our presumptive partner, and that due diligence would continue through the coming months. For Iowa Wesleyan University, the due diligence process was underscored by generative conversations the board continued to engage in regarding the future of small private colleges nationally, the role of Iowa Wesleyan in this changing landscape, the seriousness of the university's financial challenges, the indisputable importance of Iowa Wesleyan to the rural community of Mount Pleasant and Southeast Iowa, and the options for moving forward. Throughout these conversations, the board maintained a consistent focus on institutional mission and values, a dedication to professional development, adherence to best practices in strategic planning, and a deeply held commitment to underserved and under-resourced students.

Talks with Saint Leo University ultimately ended in December 2019 with both institutions realizing the merger was not in the best interests of either university. By that time, President Titus had retired, and I had stepped into the role of interim president, anticipating that the university would come under the leadership of Saint Leo's president in the near future. Our nine months of "dating" Saint Leo University were not wasted, however, as significant lessons were learned throughout the process. Perhaps readers will find a summary of those lessons helpful:

- Understand what your nonnegotiables are before entering into discussions. Are you willing to give up your institutional name? Your president or board? Your faith affiliation, if any? Will the partnership allow you to sustain your sense of purpose and mission? Remember that the more you try to hold on to, the more difficult you may find the path to a partnership or merger.
- What are the potential regulatory roadblocks? In Iowa Wesleyan's case, we found out during our due diligence process that our Iowa students would lose all access to the Iowa Tuition Grant if we merged with a Florida institution. Those grants, in an amount exceeding $6,000 annually, are a crucial piece of financial support for our regional students.
- Entering partnership discussions in order to be "saved" is not enough. A merger or partnership needs to bring something of value to each institution. There must be something in it for everyone and each institution's strengths must be recognized and incorporated. A partnership characterized by a significant imbalance in power or control may be doomed.
- If your institution contributes significantly to your region's economic landscape, how will the partnership impact that role?

Still facing serious financial challenges and insufficient enrollment in early 2020, exacerbated by the emerging global pandemic, and with time running out, the board understood the urgency of changing course quickly. The time to fill our toolbox was short. By this time, I had agreed to remain in my role to help guide the ongoing search for a partner and to ensure that the university had consistent leadership through the transitional years ahead. Thus, my designation as interim president had been changed to president.

While the initiative to merge with another university in 2019 had been driven primarily out of financial desperation, the board's subsequent year of generative discussions prepared trustees to move in a more considered direction by 2020. Through conversations with regional business and community leaders, the board and administration had educated themselves regarding the relevance of the region's economic landscape and the importance of increased educational opportunities for workforce development. The board also developed a clear understanding of the significant demographic shifts in the national higher education landscape and observed that many small private institutions faced closure. Some form of partnership with our regional community college seemed a natural approach to preparing for the future while addressing immediate concerns.

In April 2020, the board engaged the services of AGB consultants to assist with the development of a strategic rationale and financial model for a proposed affiliation with Southeastern Community College (SCC), just 30 miles from the Iowa Wesleyan campus. The intent of the affiliation was to stabilize and benefit both institutions through enrollment growth and to enhance the region's economic outlook. The two institutions have a nearly $200 million annual combined economic impact on the region. In July 2020, Iowa Wesleyan University and SCC signed a memorandum of understanding to continue due diligence and discussions toward the development of a formal affiliation agreement and contract for shared services.

As 2020 came to an end, the Iowa Wesleyan University Board of Trustees demonstrated extraordinary courage and resiliency as the spreading COVID-19 pandemic added to the university's ongoing enrollment and financial challenges. At a time when the easiest and most conservative response would have been to close the university, the IW Board instead moved forward simultaneously with four distinct key initiatives that have yielded remarkable results over the past two years, allowing the university to advance its mission as it seeks to improve the economy and the quality of life in the region. For the past three years, these initiatives have been the master tools of our trade. Central to this approach has been the formation of our alliance with Southeastern Community College.

Southeast Iowa Higher Education Alliance

In January 2021, the Southeast Iowa Higher Education Alliance (SIHEA), a unique partnership between Southeastern Community College and Iowa Wesleyan University, was formalized and publicly announced. The alliance is an innovative model for expanding access to higher education for rural students, thereby strengthening the regional workforce and economy. This unusual partnership between a public, two-year, career-focused community college and a private, four-year liberal arts university has drawn attention for its potential as a model for the future of higher education and workforce development in rural communities.

This unique partnership was a landmark outcome following a challenging process for the IW Board of Trustees. The board and administration devoted months to analyzing financial models, exploring the few existing examples of similar partnerships, and discussing possible governance structures. Discussions with the SCC Board of Directors required an understanding of the significant differences between public and private boards, an understanding the IW board took the time to develop. Claire Ramsbottom, executive director of the Colleges of the Fenway, the long-established partnership among five Boston-area institutions, was tremendously helpful in sharing that organization's bylaws and providing insight into our process.

While Iowa Wesleyan, like most four-year institutions, has many traditional articulation agreements in place with community colleges, the new SIHEA partnership is a distinctly more robust partnership—amounting to a regional educational system for Southeast Iowa. Under the agreement, a distinct new 501(c)(3) nonprofit entity, the Southeast Iowa Higher Education Alliance, was formed. IW and SCC are currently the only two members of SIHEA, although the mission and bylaws both permit and foresee the addition of associate members in the future. Such members might include regional nonprofits and social service agencies, public secondary education institutions, regional governmental agencies, or businesses. Both IW and SCC maintain their own existing governance structures, presidents, leadership teams, accreditation, and boards. SIHEA has a separate and distinct board, consisting of both institutions' presidents and two appointees of each institution, for a total of six trustees.

SIHEA's bylaws designate the president of SCC, Dr. Michael Ash, as the "chancellor" of SIHEA. While the chancellor does not have direct authority over the IW president or any IW employees, his role is to serve in an advisory capacity to the two institutions' administrative teams as they work to meet the affiliation's goals, work across the region to familiarize employers with the academic opportunities provided by SIHEA, work with community organizations to help develop strategies for the reduction of crime and poverty through education, and generally work to promote SIHEA across the region and increase visibility for both institutions.

SIHEA's bylaws outline the affiliation's mission and vision, which reflect academic and educational opportunities as well as regional workforce and community development:

Mission: The Alliance works to serve Iowa Wesleyan University and Southeastern Community College to increase enrollment; provide local educational opportunities for local students; increase retention rates of students to remain in Southeast Iowa throughout their educational journey and as they enter the workforce; enhance strategic planning and marketing efforts; create opportunities for shared expenses; engage in shared academic planning; enhance academic pathways and internships; create a less expensive bachelor's degree; and improve completion rates of each institution.

Vision: The Alliance will work to enhance regional educational opportunities and promote the growth and stability of SCC and IW through the development of academic pathways, collaborative programs, shared expenses, and fundraising initiatives, while retaining the unique qualities of SCC and IW. The Alliance works closely with regional employers to develop pathways into the workforce, and with community organizations to support regional business development.

One of the most complex challenges in the formation of our partnership has been the establishment of a workable financial model. We have focused primarily on three areas of financial emphasis. First, we worked to designate a tuition rate for students transferring from SCC to IW that would be highly competitive compared with other options for those students. The other areas of financial focus have included the establishment of a funding mechanism for the SIHEA budget to cover administrative, marketing, and other operational costs, and some form of revenue sharing to provide an incentive to SCC for promoting and supporting the alliance in order to increase transfers to IW. Our administrative teams have continued to review and modify the financial model as we gain more knowledge and experience in our recruiting methods and implementation of the partnership.

A key element in the success of our affiliation is a consistent message to SCC students and regional high school students that SIHEA is their regional higher education system. We know, of course, that IW will not be the university that meets every SCC graduate's needs. But we have significant overlap in our academic programs, making it easy to show entering SCC freshmen what their four-year pathway to a bachelor's degree will look like, whether it is in nursing, teacher education, business, criminal justice, biology, or a broad range of humanities and liberal arts options.

In addition, both IW and SCC contribute significant scholarships for SCC graduates who go on to enroll at IW for a bachelor's degree completion. These scholarships were established intentionally to ensure that over their four-year academic program through SIHEA, students will pay, on average, no more than they would have paid at a four-year state public institution. To be clear, most of IW's students are still traditional four-year students who enter as freshmen. Through SIHEA, however, we increased the enrollment of SCC transfer students significantly in our first full year of the partnership.

Our messaging to students includes not only financial incentives and clear academic pathways but language and activities that convey the depth of our partnership. Faculty and staff at both IW and SCC are encouraged to refer to the other institution as "our other campus." In the past, when IW's conditional acceptance committee evaluated applications from students who did not meet our acceptance criteria, the common advice was to suggest they return to their home and enroll at a regional community college for a year before reapplying to IW. Now, in similar circumstances, students will be advised to enroll at "our other nearby campus" (SCC) for their first two years, then take advantage of our scholarships and transfer to IW for their bachelor's degree completion.

The two institutions' offices for student development have been actively engaged in promoting our notion of a regional system. Throughout the year, numerous joint activities between the campuses ensure that SCC students have many opportunities to spend time on IW's campus and meet IW students, faculty, coaches, and staff members. These activities include intramural athletic competitions, campus entertainment opportunities such as concerts or other performances, joint shopping trips to Iowa City, and occasional joint meetings of the two student government groups. Through these activities, SCC students begin to feel that they are part of the IW community even while they are still enrolled at SCC.

Our institutions have found numerous ways to share expenses over the past year. We have shared several faculty and staff positions and are always looking for opportunities to share more. We have a shared contract with a grant writing agency in Washington, DC, and we have experimented with shared food service and campus security contracts. As the alliance grows, we will continue to look for ways to benefit from cost-sharing and enrollment growth opportunities.

One of the most rewarding aspects of our alliance has been the effort we are putting into regional community development. Specifically, this has been focused on ways to increase the numbers of regional high school graduates who pursue a postsecondary education. With the help and support of an engaged trustee, we have organized numerous meetings in communities within our surrounding counties. The story of our outreach in one community will help explain the process and results.

Keokuk is Iowa's southernmost city, in the southeast corner of the state. It is a city of about 10,000 residents, overlooking the Mississippi River. Keokuk has one of the state's highest poverty rates, with 22% of all residents living below the poverty line, including 32% of those under the age of 18. Our first meeting in Keokuk was with a group of community leaders, including individuals from the local school system, YMCA, library, labor union, day care, hospital, and others. After presenting some general information about our IW/SCC alliance, we asked these leaders how we could provide support to their community. The immediate response, in a unified voice, was "help us break the cycle of poverty." They went on to explain that college attendance is not part of the narrative for most Keokuk High School graduates and their families. There was unanimous agreement that the process of breaking the cycle of poverty must include a focus on education and changing the culture of resistance to higher education.

Every participant in that meeting presented us with a unique request relating to their work. The YMCA director said that there are typically 70 students at the YMCA after school each day, ranging from elementary through high school. He asked if we could bring some of our student athletes to the YMCA on a regular basis to spend time with these young people and introduce them to the idea of college. The library director said she spends time with young people in the community, helping them fill out job applications for local, typically low-paying jobs. She asked if we could provide her with resources and information to help students fill out college applications instead of entry-level job applications. The day care director said that she typically hires high school graduates to work at her center for a relatively low hourly wage. She asked if we could bring some of our faculty and students from our teacher education program to talk with these young employees about the option of attending college and becoming a teacher.

Our initiative in Keokuk has remained alive through continued meetings and engagement. Young people have been transported from the YMCA to the Iowa Wesleyan campus to spend a day with our athletes, enjoy a pizza party, and attend a basketball game. They have returned home sporting a new IW T-shirt, recognizing that they can comfortably be on a college campus, that they were welcomed, and that college can be part of their future. IW's student athletes have also offered several athletic camps at the Keokuk YMCA, ensuring that the engagement between students and athletes remains active. Similarly, we have introduced a SIHEA Student of the Month initiative within the Keokuk school system. Each month, a student will be selected by the middle and high school teachers to receive the SIHEA award. They will be given IW and SCC swag and be written up in the local newspaper. At the end of each semester, the honored students and their family members will be invited to a luncheon on the IW or SCC campus. Much like the athletic engagement, this provides these young people and their families with an opportunity to comfortably experience a college campus and to feel like they belong.

We have initiated a similar model in numerous other regional communities. Each community meeting allows us to hear what the challenges are in that specific area, and how our educational system can help address them. While the challenges are different in each community, increasing higher education attainment levels is nearly always part of the solution.

As we enter our second year of the partnership, we will continue to iron out wrinkles in the system. The SCC and IW administrative teams meet regularly to discuss progress, new initiatives, and challenges. The financial model remains a work in progress. The community development work is time-consuming, to the extent that there needs to be consideration of adding a SIHEA staff position for economic development. We regularly encounter culture differences between our two institutions, and these can lead to difficult conversations. Our administrative teams, however, all recognize that the outcomes are worth the difficulties, and we strive to work together to resolve our differences.

A key lesson for any institution seeking alternative pathways to financial and enrollment sustainability is that there must be numerous tools in the toolbox. In Iowa Wesleyan's case, the SIHEA partnership has been a foundational initiative that continues to change and improve. As mentioned previously, however, the board and administration also implemented three other initiatives simultaneously, each of which contributed significantly to the 25% increase in enrollment between 2019 and 2021, amid the challenging COVID-19 years.

NAIA Athletics

At a time when the COVID-19 pandemic was leading many institutions to cut athletic programs and implement coaching staff reductions as a precaution or necessity, the IW board took the risk of approving a shift back to the NAIA following a decade in NCAA Division III. The assumption made in 2011, that moving to NCAA Division III would improve the academic profile of our students, had not been borne out. Analysis of student performance over the past decade showed no change in the academic profile of incoming students. Instead, our data indicated that the academic preparedness of our new students was more than acceptable, and that the poor retention rates reflected insufficient academic supports provided by the university. This shortcoming was soon addressed through another initiative, our Student Success Center. Meanwhile, the decision to return to the NAIA proved to be a pivotal component in recruiting new students during the pandemic, while many other similar institutions were struggling to meet recruitment goals. The subsequent enrollment increases also confirmed the importance of athletic scholarships to our student athletes.

Student Success Center

Like many universities, Iowa Wesleyan strove for years to attract more "college-ready students"—those who are top performers in high school and who have low financial need. Iowa Wesleyan has chosen instead to acknowledge and embrace the population of students who actively seek out IW and thrive there—to become a "student-ready college." Iowa Wesleyan University's particular strength is providing educational opportunities and pathways for under-resourced and underserved students, including low-income and first-generation students and those from ethnically and racially diverse populations. We understand that our responsibility to our accepted students is to make sure that they have the supports in place that will allow them to succeed.

As the administration sought to expand the Student Success Center through a significant allocation of financial resources, the IW board chose to engage in substantive discussions about the university's unique niche of students. During more than one board meeting, the trustees hosted panels of faculty and students, learning through dialogue about the unique experiences of many of our students: food insecurity, dysfunctional families, urban gang violence, the role of mentors and coaches, the significance of athletics and extracurricular activities. Armed with this knowledge, the board was able to understand the administration's requests for funding and authorized a budget in 2021 that allocated significant financial resources to staffing the university's expanded Success Center. Increasing from two to eight staff members over the past year, the center now boasts four success coaches dedicated to mentoring every first-year student through the challenges that underserved students face as they enter college. In addition, the center has staff members overseeing tutoring, writing, accessibility, and other success initiatives. Overall retention rates have continued to climb as a result of these efforts.

Honors Program

In addition to allocating resources to athletic program growth and student success, the board has emphasized the continued importance of a well-rounded liberal arts program for ongoing success. As the percentage of student athletes has increased significantly, the board has pushed for continued growth in programs that provide expanded opportunities for nonathletes. Again, authorizing additional financial resources for a new initiative, the board supported the addition of the university's first Honors Program, which formally launched in the Spring 2022 semester. This program offers an honors-level curriculum across academic areas, study abroad, expanded music/theater/arts options, and opportunities for urban cultural activities.

Through the board and administration's reflective and mission-centered process amid the ongoing pandemic, Iowa Wesleyan University welcomed 347 new students in the fall semester of 2021, the largest incoming class of new students since at least 1935. Total undergraduate enrollment and total head count were the largest since 2009. Enrollment of transfer students from Southeastern Community College increased from fewer than five historically to sixteen in fall 2021, only a few months after implementing our formalized partnership. Five additional SCC students transferred in the spring of 2022, a semester that seldom draws midyear transfers. Athletic rosters have grown exponentially, and our diverse campus is a truly global community. Occupancy of residence halls is over 95%, and the university is working toward the development of new housing options for next fall.

The Iowa Wesleyan University Board of Trustees has demonstrated exemplary leadership over the past several years in the face of multiple and significant financial, enrollment, demographic, and administrative challenges, all previously existing but exacerbated by the COVID-19 pandemic. Under the guidance of an engaged and proactive board and administrative team, the university has emerged from an existential crisis to demonstrate a commitment to mission and to our students. Enrollment numbers have increased significantly. The university's successful and innovative partnership and student success initiatives have led to greatly improved retention rates and received widespread recognition. The return to the NAIA, with its character-driven focus, has served our student athletes well. Our 2021–22 athletic season yielded two women's teams that ranked with the highest and second highest GPAs in the NAIA.

Despite the pride we feel in our successes, we are aware that we will continue to face the challenges all small private colleges and universities face: the need for substantial fundraising, the need to satisfy regulatory requirements for accreditation, and the need to achieve adequate enrollment levels at a time when demographic shifts are causing a decline in the number of prospective college students. These ongoing and emerging changes to the higher education landscape will necessitate continued adaptability, but, for the moment, our toolbox is full.

As this book entered the production phase, Iowa Wesleyan University announced that it would cease operation after the Spring 2023 semester. While the partnerships developed were successful in increasing enrollment and providing an enhanced opportunity for postsecondary education in the region, the university could not reach a sustainable place. While the state of Iowa was unwilling to invest in Iowa Wesleyan as an ongoing private university, perhaps the interest of the state can lead to an alternative future for this important mission of preparing rural students in rural areas to serve rural communities.

CHAPTER FOUR

A Strategic Partnership

Necessity Is the Mother of Invention

PAUL BALDASARE JR.

Past President, St. Andrews University

IN EARLY DECEMBER 2006, St. Andrews Presbyterian College (now St. Andrews University) found itself facing an institutional crisis. At that time, St. Andrews was at the end of its first year of probationary status with its regional accrediting agency, the Southern Association of Colleges and Schools (SACSOC), for not complying with a core requirement of accreditation to demonstrate a sound financial base to support the college's mission. At its annual December meeting, SACSOC reaffirmed that the college's mission, academic and cocurricular programs, its successful fundraising, and its other administrative unit plans and assessments met—and remarkably exceeded—SACSOC's overall requirements for accreditation notwithstanding the college's limited resources. However, SACSOC found that St. Andrews was still not in compliance with its financial resources core requirement and continued St. Andrews on probation for an additional six months, rather than the normally expected full second year. It demanded that the college do two things: (1) develop a "satisfactory" five-year financial management plan and (2) reduce significantly its external debt so the college's debt-to-equity financial ratios at the end of the fiscal year in May would meet the unique standard that SACSOC had developed and prescribed for its member institutions.

In response to SACSOC, and with deep concern for the college's future and the impact on the local community, the St. Andrews Board of Trustees held an emergency meeting several days after receiving the SACSOC report. It asked for, and immediately received, the resignation of the college's president, who was in the sixth year of his presidency and for some time had been experiencing the diminished confidence of the board. Two days before Christmas, the board chair and members of the executive committee asked me to become the eighth president of St. Andrews Presbyterian College. For the preceding nine years, I had served as the vice president for institutional advancement at my *alma mater* and had recently led the advancement staff in successfully completing a $36 million Share the Vision campaign for St. Andrews. With my acceptance of the presidency, neither I nor the trustees, nor anyone else for that matter, could have realized that in little more than six months the college would begin four years of life-threatening federal litigation with SACSOC. This litigation would ultimately result in a court-ordered negotiated settlement leading to an unprecedented partnership with another small, private SACSOC-accredited university 565 miles away from Laurinburg, North Carolina, in the small town of Babson Park, Florida.

The college's journey to establish a partnership, rather than a merger, with another accredited school was circuitous, fraught with uncertainty, severely challenged by the worst economic recession since the Great Depression, and complicated by the different goals and aspirations of the two partner institutions traveling together in uncharted territory. This history is one full of creative problem-solving and some successes, but also some missed opportunities and failures. Most rewarding for me was witnessing the extraordinary perseverance and support of the trustees, faculty, staff, alumni, the Presbyterian Church (USA), and the small community of Laurinburg that all cherished St. Andrews.

The Partners

St. Andrews University, notably, was formed by the merger of two Presbyterian-related colleges—Flora MacDonald College in Red Springs, North Carolina (founded for women in 1896) and Presbyterian Junior College for Men in Maxton, North Carolina (founded in 1928). Initially known as Consolidated Presbyterian College, the new school was chartered in 1958. Following three years of construction and program development, the new college was named St. Andrews Presbyterian College and instruction began in 1961 as a residential, coeducational, senior college of arts and sciences in Laurinburg, North Carolina.

Throughout its history, St. Andrews has been known for its innovative programs and its student-centered focus on the development of the whole person—intellectually, socially, and spiritually. Over the years, three innovations brought the college considerable distinction. From its beginning, St. Andrews pioneered in serving the educational needs of students with physical disabilities, with a campus designed and constructed to be largely barrier-free. Its highly interdisciplinary, team-taught general education program in both the liberal arts and the sciences originally known as Christianity and Culture (C&C), later changed to St. Andrews General Education (SAGE), was widely recognized for its innovation and quality. And beginning in the 1980s, the development of a comprehensive equestrian program that combined both academic programs and competitive riding, that today is housed at a 300-acre equestrian center, gained the school wide recognition as having one of the best equestrian programs in the country.

Webber International University, located in Babson Park, Florida, was founded in 1927 by Roger Babson, an entrepreneur and business theorist, as a two-year school for women named Webber College. It was one of the first business schools for women in the United States but today is a four-year institution that hosts men and women from some 48 different nations on its residential campus. At the time of these discussions, Webber was primarily a business school offering associate's degrees and bachelor's degrees in business, accounting, management, and finance, with additional majors concentrating on hospitality, sports and criminal justice management. At the time, it had recently begun offering a master's degree in business. Over the years, Webber gained a very favorable reputation internationally with its programs designed to attract students from around the world.

From inception, St. Andrews and Webber have always been nonprofit 501(c)(3) charitable organizations and accredited by SACSOC. Both schools had enrollments of fewer than 1,000, both had active sports programs—St. Andrews a member of NCAA Division II and Webber a member of the NAIA—both had fledgling online programs, and each struggled in a variety of ways to increase enrollment and improve retention year over year. While St. Andrews had a strong, long-standing, unrestricted fundraising program, which it relied on to help meet its expenses, Webber relied solely on tuition, room, board, and auxiliary revenue to balance its budget each year.

How It All Began: A Matter of Necessity

At my inauguration as president of St. Andrews during our annual Alumni Weekend in April 2007, I stressed in my remarks that the future of private, church-related higher education in general, and for St. Andrews in particular, depended on developing "strategic alliances, collaborations and partnerships to extend our academic offerings and cocurricular opportunities for our students and faculty." I also noted how essential these types of relationships could be to our long-term growth and financial security. A short two months later, in June 2007, our accreditation agency notified us by letter that it was stripping St. Andrews of its accreditation for failure to meet the agency's financial core requirement, but without giving St. Andrews the normal two full years of probationary status. This was particularly perplexing and alarming because we had demonstrated in our report to SACSOC that St. Andrews was current with its creditors, meeting its payroll and vendor obligations, and anticipating a larger entering class for the upcoming fall term as well as improved retention of current students.

Under these dire circumstances, we immediately appealed the SACSOC decision and filed suit in federal district court. We quickly secured an injunction to prevent the loss of federal financial aid for our students pending the outcome of our lawsuit. We then embarked on a legal journey with a cloud hanging over our head and costing us millions of dollars. At the time, we had no idea that the litigation would take more than four years and would conclude with a last-minute negotiation of a partnership agreement to secure our accreditation and continued existence as a regionally accredited private college.

At the start of the litigation, we took one of the most important steps for any institution considering a strategic partnership or merger— forced or otherwise—we hired highly regarded professionals in several key areas to help us. We retained both excellent local legal counsel and a national expert in higher education law to represent the college. At various times, we also hired certified public accountants well versed in nonprofit accounting and finance. Finally, in preparing for a worst outcome from litigation, we entered into a contractual relationship with an expert consultant in higher education operations and regulatory compliance. Perhaps most importantly, the consultant was very experienced in higher education partnerships, mergers, and acquisitions.

Our consultant was remarkably creative and tireless in his efforts to help St. Andrews identify and structure relationships with other schools that would help meet SACSOC requirements and at the same time maintain the college's identity as a church-related, liberal arts and science college. He also advised on new academic initiatives the college could explore in order to make it more appealing to potential partners. Although our relationship with him did not extend through to our relationship with Webber, his ideas and structural guidance informed the kernel of the relationship we ultimately described in the memorandum of understanding and then implemented in the definitive agreement between St. Andrews and Webber. The structure we developed had never been seen or approved by SACSOC before, but it proved to meet all of SACSOC requirements and remains today a unique arrangement between two schools.

In our litigation, a federal district court judge in Atlanta in September 2009 ruled in favor of SACSOC, citing a federal court of appeals decision involving another decision by SACSOC to strip the accreditation of a small private college in Tennessee. This appellate decision, entered less than a year before our final hearing in the district court, essentially held that membership in a regional accrediting body is a voluntary association by the member schools. As such, the accrediting agency is free to establish whatever rules its members approve, provided the agency follows its own procedures and processes in implementing the rules. Fortunately, the district court judge expressed displeasure that SACSOC had not followed his order to provide St. Andrews with all the documents it had appropriately requested in the discovery process. With that decision made, St. Andrews immediately filed a motion for sanctions against SACSOC and appealed the judge's final decision on the merits of the case to the Eleventh Circuit Court of Appeals. Under federal rules, the appellate court ordered both parties to participate in mandatory mediation before the case could proceed on appeal.

Throughout the litigation, SACSOC had refused to discuss any type of settlement with St. Andrews. However, once the district court judge made his ruling and St. Andrews filed motions to appeal the decision and seek sanctions against SACSOC for failure to comply with discovery orders, SACSOC was suddenly very interested in discussing some type of settlement. After several months of mediation, SACSOC agreed to remain bound by the injunction and maintain St. Andrews' accreditation for one year to give St. Andrews time to partner with another accredited school in order to fall within that school's "accreditation umbrella." In exchange, St. Andrews agreed to drop its motion for sanctions that would limit the negative publicity associated with SACSOC violation of the district court's discovery order. With that agreement finalized in 2010, our trustees, senior administrative colleagues, and I redoubled our efforts to find another school with which to partner in a structure and manner that would meet the agreed-upon settlement terms with SACSOC.

Goals and Challenges

Prior to and during the one-year accreditation grace period afforded by the settlement, we met with presidents and school representatives of more than 30 colleges and universities to present the case for a partnership that would preserve St. Andrews' accreditation. With the active support of St. Andrews trustees, most notably our board chair, we made presentations to these other schools. In those presentations, we explained the history of St. Andrews, its current financial and enrollment challenges coming out of a very public dispute with its accrediting agency, and the potential benefits that would accrue to both the prospective partner and to St. Andrews.

From the outset, our goals were multifaceted, but first and foremost was to establish a relationship with another school that would ensure the college's regional accreditation and therefore secure our students' eligibility for federal financial aid. It was equally important to me as an alum—and to all of our constituents—that the college's name, identity, mission, church-relatedness, and separate corporate existence be maintained to the greatest extent possible. But it was clear that a new partnership would have to include changes to address the most significant challenges the college had been experiencing for a number of years: under-enrollment, weak retention, limited finances, and the need for new and more marketable academic and cocurricular programs.

In the course of networking widely with other college presidents, higher education consultants, leaders of independent college and university organizations, and even educational entrepreneurs, we continued to run into roadblocks because of St. Andrews' weakened financial position, its remote rural location, and its sullied reputation created in large measure by SACSOC's public actions and our disputed litigation. Many of the schools located in the Southern Association region confidentially expressed reluctance to get involved for fear of creating their own problems with SACSOC given the high level of scrutiny that SACSOC would have over whatever relationship St. Andrews and a partner school developed.

A constant challenge throughout our litigation and during discussions with potential partners was the question of confidentiality versus transparency with the college's many constituents, each requiring a different level of "need to know." We made the decision early on that regular communication, and transparency to the greatest extent possible, was essential to keep down unfounded rumors and at the same time build support for whatever legal result and partnership relationship would emerge. During the litigation, we kept our trustees and senior staff fully informed about the court case, our legal strategies, timelines for decisions, and possible outcomes. We also gave faculty and staff updates at regularly scheduled meetings, and at times specially called meetings, when court decisions on motions and final hearings were made. With court decisions being a matter of public record, we made every effort to get the word out to all constituents prior to the court decision hitting the public record. We were fortunate to also have a senior staff and a faculty executive committee with which I could speak frankly about the litigation and rely on the members to maintain confidentiality when required but also serve as consistent, supportive communicators to their faculty and staff colleagues.

Once the court had made its decision, we were in a grace period with SACSOC under court protection to find a partner school. In virtually all of our significant discussions with potential partners, nondisclosure agreements were agreed upon before meaningful discussions could even begin. At this point, transparent communication with college constituents became even more important. Most of our discussions with potential partners took place at locations away from campus, but we made it clear in varying degrees of detail to our constituents that we were exploring a wide array of potential relationships that could result in satisfying SACSOC and the court while remaining true to our mission and identity. During this entire period of litigation and partner shopping, we had to communicate a balance of hope and optimism with the serious realities of our very fragile situation. In retrospect, I am glad that our team leaned into transparency, but I'm sure at times we were more hopeful and positive than warranted on the one hand, and discouraging and less than confident of the future on the other hand. However, all of us agreed that our effort to be as transparent as possible paid dividends over time and created trust and confidence that we were doing all that we could to resolve this existential threat.

The Plan and the Partnership

Following our unsuccessful discussions with more than 30 potential partners, I had the opportunity to meet with a successful educational investor in Atlanta. During the course of our discussion, he mentioned to me a small school in Florida he had looked at a year or so earlier that had an entrepreneurial spirit and might have an interest in talking to me about some sort of relationship for our two schools. The school he mentioned was Webber International University. Coincidentally, but not on my radar at the time, the president of Webber was a St. Andrews alum who graduated a decade after I graduated. While I had never met him, I had written him a short note of congratulations several years earlier when he was named president of Webber.

Frustrated by our inability to find a suitable partner and conscious of the diminishing time remaining to find a partner willing to take the next steps to reach an agreement, we contacted Webber's president. With his very favorable experience as a student at St. Andrews and his openness to new ideas, he agreed to meet with us to discuss possibilities. He made no commitment, however, to do anything more than listen to the case we were making for some type of relationship that would salvage St. Andrews' accreditation and to the greatest extent possible benefit Webber. In our earliest discussions, it became clear that we shared some basic goals, and that our individual goals for our schools were not necessarily inconsistent with one another.

In our earliest conversations, we very quickly reached an understanding that there was great potential for a partnership that would enable both schools to do the following:

- Work together to find cost savings in every area of operations, including purchasing, sharing employees, consolidating some back-office operations, and enhancing our respective academic programs at little additional cost.
- Create streamlined opportunities for students on both campuses to take courses in person and remotely, at no additional cost, on each other's campus.

- Focus efforts on student retention by expanding course offerings in combination with one another and opening up cocurricular experiences, such as study abroad and semester-long study on each other's campus.
- Share best practices, especially in the area of new student recruitment, athletics, financial aid packaging, and financial management.
- Most importantly, secure SACSOC approval for this unique relationship that would preserve St. Andrews' accreditation while at the same time provide maximum liability protection for Webber.

With these shared overarching goals, we began working in earnest to create a structure and operational relationship that on paper would provide a framework for success. Fortunately, from the very beginning of our discussions, Webber's president and trustees made it clear that they had no interest in a partnership that would result in Webber becoming a liberal arts and sciences school, nor would they want St. Andrews to become a business school. They were completely comfortable with both schools remaining true to their educational missions.

They valued their history as a business school but saw an opportunity in higher education to join several small, boutique colleges with distinctive missions and academic strengths into a structured relationship that would "raise all ships." This idea was modeled on the health care industry in which large urban hospitals were creating health care systems comprised of community-based hospitals into one interrelated system of health care. One of Webber's trustees had been particularly successful in the health care industry building exactly this kind of system.

As we continued to discuss the possibilities, both presidents and boards identified specific opportunities for cost savings and containment for our schools through joint purchasing of supplies and especially technology, rather than acting separately. We considered the possibility of sharing the skills of certain key staff members and the use of operating systems that could serve both campuses. We looked at ways to give students more opportunities to take courses at the other campus in person or remotely, thereby expanding the availability of courses and majors beyond what either school could offer independently. And from a retention point of view, we explored how we could market each other's campus and programs to those students who were not happy at one school, or who had decided to change their academic focus but could be persuaded to consider "transferring" to the other school without loss of course credits and still be able to graduate on time. And finally, we began identifying systems and ways of doing things that could be presented to the other campus as "best practices" using our own subject matter experts from each other's campus for training purposes without the cost of outside consultants.

Several opportunities were of particularly strong interest to both parties. St. Andrews, for example, had a long history of successful fundraising with systems, technology, and experienced development and alumni affairs professionals firmly in place. We believed we could share best fundraising practices with Webber, which had no recent history of a fundraising program.

On the other hand, Webber had a quality accounting major and master's program in business administration. With advice and a solid programmatic structure, Webber could export to St. Andrews these programs to expand its own modest business major and be an opportunity to offer liberal arts and sciences master's programs on its campus. Webber also had been very intentional in its efforts to recruit international students and would be able to help St. Andrews grow its student population by sharing Webber's international student recruitment plans and techniques.

With regard to the primary goal of securing SACSOC approval for our plan, we were fortunate that Webber's president and staff had worked closely with SACSOC on Webber's own accreditation and had developed strong, trustworthy relationships with key staff at SACSOC. This, in combination with both campuses being blessed with talented individual staff and faculty members well versed in accreditation compliance, made our institutional effectiveness and compliance systems on both campuses and our written submissions to SACSOC to be of the very highest quality. St. Andrews had a faculty member who had worn many administrative hats, including his appointment to serve as vice president of institutional effectiveness and research shortly after I became president. Not long after, Webber hired a new member of its staff who was a highly talented teacher and administrator and very experienced in navigating the interrelated regulatory labyrinth of programmatic review and reaccreditation.

In short, from the outset of our discussions, we both saw opportunities to strengthen our two campuses with programs, personnel, and resources that could be shared at limited cost and yet have a positive impact on operations and revenue growth at both schools.

Challenges to Partnership

In the face of these potential benefits for both schools, there were challenges—real and imagined—that made it difficult to move forward from good-spirited, well-intended conversations to more focused, serious discussions and due diligence. Rightly so, some of Webber's trustees were skeptical from the beginning of any arrangement with a school of similar size and modest endowment as well as marginal finances that both schools were currently experiencing. In other words, will two struggling schools be stronger together, or will the new partner drag the other under from the sheer weight of its difficulties? Looming in the background throughout the discussions was the concern that after the expenditure of considerable time, energy, and resources by both schools, SACSOC might not approve whatever substantive change we put forward for consideration.

The biggest obstacle to moving forward was financial. Webber's trustees and its president were most concerned about our ability to structure an agreement that would provide complete liability protection for Webber from any and all St. Andrews obligations—current and in the future. Webber was willing to help us out and gain some benefits from the relationship, but it would not provide any funding, acquire any assets, take on any long-term debt obligations, or incur additional vendor obligations to make the relationship work.

The proposed structure would have to legally insulate Webber from St. Andrews' liabilities *and* meet SACSOC's accreditation requirements. But in addition, the plan would also have to be approved by the US Department of Education; the secretaries of state for North Carolina and Florida; the North Carolina State Education Assistance Authority, which oversees the distribution of NC financial aid to NC students attending NC private colleges and universities; the NCAA and NAIA; St. Andrews' creditors; and our respective state private colleges and associations.

In broad strokes, the key terms we agreed upon were to maintain the separate nonprofit, 501(c)(3) corporate identities of each school but to change the St. Andrews corporation from a North Carolina nonmembership corporation to a North Carolina membership corporation and name Webber as the sole member. As the sole member, Webber would have the specific fiduciary responsibility to appoint the members of the St. Andrews Board of Trustees. With preapproval from SACSOC, this unique structure satisfied its requirement that the accredited entity—Webber International University—and its board of trustees had ultimate authority over St. Andrews through its power to appoint its governing board. Although not proposed in the initial substantive change submission nor required in SACSOC's approval, Webber and St. Andrews agreed to populate both boards of trustees with some members of the former Webber and former St. Andrews boards, but with the Webber trustees in the majority on both boards.

In addition, both schools, in their own names,[1] would contract separately with vendors, submit their own federal and state tax filings, file independent federal demographic reports, maintain separate websites, and, except in the narrow area of federal financial aid, act as independent corporations holding separate but coordinated board meetings. Webber provided no guarantees on any St. Andrews debt or other obligations. St. Andrews remained the employer of record for all faculty and staff on the St. Andrews campus, with its own health care and retirement plans and subject to North Carolina corporate laws as a North Carolina private college. Webber would do the same as a Florida corporation and employer.

While there were other changes made to satisfy St. Andrews creditors and other regulatory bodies, maintaining separate corporate identities was the key to solving the accreditation issue for St. Andrews while at the same time insulating Webber from any and all St. Andrews liabilities, with the exception of possible future federal financial aid obligations. With this corporate structure in place and with SACSOC, US Department of Education, and NCSEAA approvals, we were able to formalize our relationship in September 2011 in time to meet SACSOC's and the federal court's modestly extended grace period for this partnership to be completed.

As with most best-laid plans, there are surprises and unanticipated consequences. The first surprise and major disruption came when the NCAA refused to allow St. Andrews to maintain its NCAA membership unless Webber agreed to apply for its own membership in the NCAA. Webber had a long and satisfactory history as a member of the NAIA and had no interest in changing athletic associations. The NCAA's decision was particularly surprising and frustrating because we had met with the NCAA staff on more than one occasion prior to completing the partnership to explain why we were structuring the relationship in the way that we did. We were led to believe that they understood what we were doing and tacitly approved of it.

However, as soon as we completed the agreements between our two schools and had final SACSOC and US Department of Education approvals, the NCAA told us that its "staff" had decided that St. Andrews no longer met NCAA requirements because our accreditation was tied to Webber's accreditation and Webber was not a member of the NCAA. With so many student athletes on our campus, the loss of an athletic association home would have resulted in nearly 100 student athletes leaving St. Andrews. Fortunately, the NAIA leadership went out of its way to fast-track St. Andrews' membership application and probationary status so that our student athletes could continue to compete in intercollegiate athletics, albeit in a new association, a new conference, and with an entirely new set of schools with which to compete.

The Honeymoon

As with any new relationship, especially one that made survival possible, the first reaction on the St. Andrews campus was a feeling of tremendous relief and a renewed sense of optimism in the future. What initially worked well at the beginning quickly became the new normal. Differences in campus culture and management styles, however, became more apparent and difficult to navigate as time went on. As a business school, not surprisingly, Webber operated more like a traditional for-profit corporation. Management was much more hierarchical and decision-making centralized among the president and a small circle of senior staff with minimal involvement of faculty, lower-level staff, and students. During the period of discussion and due diligence, Webber's faculty, staff, alumni, and its local community were unaware that a partnership with another school was even being contemplated. Under its management style, information and discussions about institutional changes, opportunities, or difficulties were held to that very small circle of trustees and senior staff until such time as an announcement was made, if announced at all. The need-to-know was very limited and absolute confidentiality was required and paramount.

Webber's 14-member board of trustees and its committees were structured to focus almost exclusively on investment oversight, budget approval, and other matters of finance, with little engagement on academic and cocurricular matters. Regularly scheduled board meetings were held twice a year and typically lasted only a few hours with an occasional short interim meeting at the end of the first semester or the end of the academic year. Communication and interaction of board members with faculty, staff, and students were not a part of board meetings, although local trustees frequently attended athletic events and other activities on the Webber campus. Membership on the Webber board was comprised primarily of Floridians, many of whom were local business leaders, and a few were also alumni.

As a liberal arts and science undergraduate college, St. Andrews operated more like a traditional academic institution. The ideal of shared governance with faculty was an important, helpful, valued, and long-standing commitment of the college's board and administration. Management and decision-making were collaborative and collegial in ways commonly found for generations at many private colleges. St. Andrews' 36-member board of trustees met three times a year, with each meeting lasting two days and including an evening dinner on the first day, at which trustees had the opportunity to socialize with faculty, staff, and students. The board operated with a committee structure that included Committees on Academic Affairs, Student Life and Athletics, Budget and Finance, Enrollment Management, and Audit. A special Committee on Trustees focused on the recruitment of new trustees and the annual evaluation of the board and the president. Selected faculty members and students were always included in committee meetings to offer insights and perspective on the committees' particular areas of responsibility. Transparency was valued and as a result confidentiality was understood to be necessary at times, but with the further understanding that information would be shared as widely as possible and as soon as possible. Membership on the board consisted of representatives of the college's various constituencies—alumni, Presbyterian church leaders, local community leaders, parents of students or recent graduates, and major donors, with special attention paid to gender and geographical diversity.

Once the partnership was completed, both board meetings were structured the way Webber's board was accustomed to meeting, and major management decisions for both campuses grew increasingly centralized. While these organizational, leadership, and management differences were not major impediments in the early years of the relationship, they did, over time, create some miscommunications and misunderstandings for faculty, staff, and students. In the early years, there was little interaction between the two campuses, with the exception of senior management. With 500-plus miles between campuses, senior management on both campuses met once a week via Skype, and eventually Zoom, in order to keep in touch, discuss new initiatives, troubleshoot areas of concern, begin the process of harmonizing operational processes, and share best practices with one another. Webber's president made an effort to visit the St. Andrews campus at least once every few months, and several members of the St. Andrews management team, myself included, visited the Webber campus. Both boards alternated meeting on each campus with the hope that all of the trustees would get familiar with the culture, campus facilities, local community, and unique challenges and opportunities on each campus. Unfortunately, the distance between the campuses and the short meeting schedules resulted in many of the trustees calling or zooming into meetings rather than attending in person.

Given the unusual circumstances forcing St. Andrews to seek a partnership with another school in order to survive, the relationship created was essentially successful for both St. Andrews and Webber. For St. Andrews, it solved its accreditation challenge while allowing it to maintain its mission, its identity, and, for the most part, its campus culture. For Webber, it gave the school an opportunity to take the first step in putting together what its leadership believed would be a distinctive and stronger model for small private colleges to band together under an overarching management structure. The hopes were high that this would allow each institution to benefit from sharing resources while maintaining their own unique attraction.

With this overarching success, however, many fundamental differences made the relationship less successful than it might otherwise have been. Specifically:

- The distance between the two campuses made it difficult to create genuine camaraderie and a sense of shared purpose among the faculties and staffs. In some respects, it was "out of sight, out of mind."
- The physical plant size and maintenance differences, as well as the very different programmatic needs of the two schools, were difficult for each party to fully appreciate. The financial needs of a multidisciplinary liberal arts college compared to an essentially single-discipline business college made working together especially challenging. Leadership and the board at Webber had a difficult time understanding and supporting the need for a larger faculty and staff and related expenses at a liberal arts and

sciences institution with a sprawling 200-acre main campus and a 300-acre equestrian center compared to its single-focused business school situated on a relatively small, compact campus.

- Containing costs and developing cost-effective and smooth vendor relationships required an understanding of the differences in long-standing and favorable local relationships in NC for St. Andrews compared to the same type of relationships in Florida for Webber. The learning curve to understand and appreciate the very different operational needs at each campus was quite steep. In many ways, attempting to consolidate management positions in business and finance, enrollment management, and faculty leadership was nearly impossible given the significant differences between the two campuses.

- The different approaches to management and governance—centralized at Webber and more decentralized and collaborative at St. Andrews—at times created misunderstandings and undercut the "buy-in" by faculty and staff most needed to implement the goals of the partnership. The different communication styles of leadership on each campus sometimes made it difficult to balance the desire of leadership on the Webber campus to keep information closely held and limited to a small circle of senior administrators, compared to the more transparent, shared governance, and decentralized leadership approach on the St. Andrews campus. These differences at times created misunderstandings, unfortunate surprises, and at times a lack of trust in leadership.

- Finally, the fact that both partners were financially challenged, struggled with under-enrollment, had student retention issues, and had small overworked professional staffs in all areas of operations meant that there was little time, energy, and resources available to put toward the needs of the partnership to make it more operationally successful.

Lessons Learned

As I closed out my presidency in 2020 and reflected on the opportunities for successful partnerships, strategic alliances, and mergers in higher education, several "lessons learned" for me stand out.

- Start as early as possible to explore the possibilities, or eventual necessity, of a partnership, strategic alliance, or merger; don't wait for a crisis to occur. Build this exploration into your long-range planning process as one of many options available to strengthen your institution for the long run.
- Campus culture does matter. If the cultures of two schools considering a partnership, merger, or acquisition are significantly different, it is very difficult to create a new culture that will be shared on both campuses.
- Transparent and consistent communication to all stakeholders is essential. For a partnership to be supported and celebrated by those who labor at the schools, by the students who are there to learn, and by the many constituents who care deeply about their schools, communication must be clear, frank, open, and neither overly optimistic nor deadly pessimistic.
- As soon as possible, retain the services of the very best, most experienced professionals—attorneys, accountants, consultants —the school can afford to guide trustees and management through the process of a strategic partnership or merger. The right professionals can help streamline the process, raise important questions early, avoid major pitfalls, and provide different relationship models that can be tailored to meet each school's most important goals.
- Decision-making that is collegial, collaborative, and respectful of those up and down the organizational chart will garner better decisions and stronger campus-wide support in the long run than top-down directives. Trust in leadership will make the inevitability of change much easier to implement and to support.

- The institutional mission and the quality of the student experience at each campus should be the touchstones in every decision that leadership makes. Both partners, however, have to recognize that the quality of student experience may be different from one campus to the other depending on the nature of the particular academic and cocurricular programs offered and the traditions and expectations that faculty, staff, and students hold dear.
- While access to financial resources is critically important to success, equally important is the leadership of informed and engaged trustees, the demonstrated trustworthiness of senior management, and an open-minded and creative attitude of full-time faculty and staff.

Conclusion

The circumstances under which St. Andrews was forced to pursue a strategic relationship with another school were unusual, and far from ideal, in comparison to other successfully planned and implemented higher education partnerships and mergers. Faced with a deadly ultimatum by a third-party regulator, and with relatively little time to put all the pieces together in a well-orchestrated, strategically planned relationship, the St. Andrews–Webber partnership was remarkably successful at meeting its immediate short-term goals. St. Andrews was able to stave off a loss of accreditation, and Webber was able to explore a new model in higher education by joining two small colleges with distinctive missions under one managerial umbrella without incurring additional liabilities. In short, the relationship between the two schools was initially successful.

But the prospect for long-term success remains to be seen. The institutions' very different histories, missions, campus cultures, styles of governance, and leadership in the face of a rapidly changing higher education marketplace are not necessarily compatible with one another. A one-size-fits-all, centralized approach to problem-solving, student recruitment, cost containment, and revenue production at a multidisciplinary, residential campus with students from across the country no doubt will prove to be very different than for a college with one primary disciplinary focus with most of its students from its home state. How the two institutions work together to address similar problems and opportunities, and more importantly work to support each other in pursuing their own unique educational goals and aspirations, will tell the tale of their future together in the years to come.

1. For several months following SACSOC approval of the partnership, SACSOC was unclear how to name the relationship between Webber and St. Andrews. The partnership did not fit squarely into SACSOC's definitions of an additional instructional location, a branch, or an affiliate. After a great deal of discussion with SACSOC officials, SACSOC finally determined to call St. Andrews a branch campus of Webber and required that all St. Andrews publications, communications, letterhead, signage, and other formal public references use the following language: St. Andrews University, a branch of Webber International University.

CHAPTER FIVE

Better Together

Imaginative Integration

MABLENE KRUEGER

Past President, Robert Morris University Illinois

"You'll Never Work Again"

These words were stated to me by a good friend and longtime higher education consultant when I confidentially discussed with him the opportunity Robert Morris University Illinois (RMUI) was contemplating. These were hardly the words I wanted to hear, as a xx-year-old woman who was supporting an ex-husband and daughter in grad school. I understand what he meant, though. What higher education entity would desire a leader who was unable or unwilling to stay independent? What is lurking in the background that made this happen? Would they do the same with another university? We know most colleges and universities are thinking about this (or they should be), yet most are afraid to say it out loud.

This discussion has led me on a quest to talk about this transaction every chance I get: to share the background, the people, the timing, and the strategy . . . and to now highlight outcomes that were made possible because we did exactly this, with an effective date of March 10, 2020. Yes, Roosevelt University acquired Robert Morris University Illinois, where I was an alum, a 40-year member of the faculty/staff, and the sitting president. It happened a week before businesses were forced to move to remote in Chicago because of the COVID-19 pandemic, unbeknownst to us at the time.

Missions and Strategic Plans

Robert Morris University Illinois was a small, secular, private not-for-profit, one that had grown explosively in the 20-year span from 1980 to 2000 by adding campus locations, new degrees and degree levels, and athletics. We were centered from our inception in the 1970s on career-focused programming, preparing predominantly first-generation college students for the world of work. Our mission was to offer career-focused degrees to a diverse student body in a collegiate environment. We grew from offering associate's degrees to bachelor's in the 1990s. We added the master's level during my time as provost and at our peak had more than 6,000 students at 10 locations, with the flagship campus in the Chicago loop. We were an HSI (Hispanic-Serving Institution, a federal designation), with approximately one-third of our students being Caucasian, one-third African American, and one-third Hispanic. The majority of our students, typically 70%-plus, were PELL eligible, designated by the federal government as those in extreme need of financial assistance; most qualified for a state of Illinois need-based award as well. Approximately 30% were student athletes; close to half of our first-year enrollment had an athletic record at the time we merged.

Roosevelt University is a private, secular NFP with a strong social justice mission, living out its historic beginnings when the president and faculty walked out of another college when asked to report on and set quotas by ethnicity. "We don't count that way" is boldly stated throughout the university. Its strong liberal arts programs and bachelor's through doctoral degree offerings allow it to have comprehensive programming. It also boasts a conservatory music and theater performing arts college. A new, beautiful vertical campus building was completed in 2012, with the top 15 of 30 floors designated as residence halls overlooking the city of Chicago and Lake Michigan.

Both universities had grown rapidly in the 1980s and 1990s and were experiencing stress by 2015. The pressure came from multiple directions. The high school student numbers in Illinois and throughout the Midwest were rapidly declining and expected to continue to do so for the next two decades. The state of Illinois and the federal government were not keeping pace with student needs and the increased cost of education. Furthermore, real estate in the city of Chicago, with a physical presence in an accessible urban area imperative to serve our collective students, is expensive. Although the Chicago Public Schools were graduating a higher percentage of students than in the past, their numbers were rapidly decreasing. Roosevelt's construction of its vertical campus resulted in high debt; Robert Morris had multiple long-term leases with some limited flexibility over the next ten years. By 2018, enrollment at each university was 50–75% of what it was at its highest. Long-term health was at stake.

Roosevelt University appointed President Ali Malekzadeh to office in July 2015. He quickly and ferociously worked with the board to center the strategic plan on searching for appropriate colleges to acquire. Robert Morris had elected me as president that same month and year, after I had served as the provost for the past 15. Our strategic plan was built around partnerships. We had a successful history of working with partners from the community for space, programming, and strategic initiatives. The discussions I began having with the RMUI Board in 2016 were focused on acquiring and creating alliances while hinting at searching for an appropriate acquirer.

Primarily, it was and remains quite easy to see the complementarity of missions. Roosevelt University's strong roots and belief in social justice provided a natural umbrella for Robert Morris University Illinois's mission of social equity. We had pain points in common, revolving around real estate. RMUI began a consolidation of its campuses in 2016, made possible through expiring leases and selling a few owned buildings. We had little long-term debt and were able to utilize much of our small endowment to pay off most of it. However, the flagship location had a 20-year lease that could not be restructured until at least 2025.

RU, on the other hand, had high debt resulting from the construction of a beautiful vertical campus building in downtown Chicago that included performance space, residence halls, classrooms, and offices. Roosevelt's endowment was more than $100 million and growing, then to more than $160 million.

What began as a collegial discussion over breakfast about how we might do some things together (I was interested in utilizing some of RU's advanced science and math classes for RMUI's students) resulted quickly in discovering that we had an opportunity to extend both our legacies. We could offer our students greater choice and service by becoming one university under the Roosevelt name, a strong presence we could grow nationally and even internationally.

Of significant importance at this point and throughout the integration planning and implementation was the working relationship between the two presidents. Beginning in 2015, we had become friends and began to trust one another. We were both active in many of the same organizations, formally and informally. Although each of us had talked with other presidents about partnering in numerous ways, this particular transaction began to take shape as the number one opportunity.

Choices Are Important

From the first conversations with President Ali, working with him to determine the best way for RU to acquire Robert Morris University Illinois seemed optimum. However, I continued to work on other options for the future of RMUI. These included a tireless multiyear goal of renegotiating our lease obligations, including meeting with city of Chicago leaders about our tax exposure. Although we were an NFP, since we leased space, we paid high and escalating city taxes passed through in our lease, increasing as much as $1 million per year. Naturally, we searched for additional or alternative funding sources while also continuing to grow enrollment in a dwindling market.

But First, What About the Board of Trustees?

Because of my longevity at RMUI, when I officially became president in 2015, I was aware of impending long-term stress. Our mission was vulnerable; we were unsure if it could be preserved. From the very beginning of my presidency, I began working with our board of 14 members to confidently move toward a brighter future. Many were long-time board members (30-plus years), with the most recent being added a few years earlier. Naturally, the members with more experience had an allegiance to our former president, who remained on the board but was not active. Our conversations began with a review of the current demographics and changes in the Midwest, our mission/legacy, and a 10-year projection based on these facts. "Hope is not a strategy" is a statement I repeated at every meeting. The result of that work, over a year's time, was twofold: (1) some board members decided not to renew their term, and (2) those who understood and elected to stay agreed we had three options:

1. Change our business model
2. Acquire other universities/colleges
3. Become acquired by a larger university/college

Over the following two years, I worked concurrently on all three. We signed nondisclosure agreements with more than one college but did not find the right fit to acquire. I worked tirelessly to fundraise, renegotiate leases (including considering purchasing our building), lower our tax exposure, and increase revenue. At each quarterly board meeting, I laid out where we were with each item and asked the board to approve continued work. They were energetic, involved, and helpful. Truthfully, though, I was concerned. We had 12 board members for the last year, which was the minimum our bylaws dictated. While I didn't want to add more at this stage of our existence, I also couldn't afford to lose any.

The decision to become acquired by Roosevelt University was neither a first choice nor one of desperation. Rather, it emerged over time as an optimum way to extend our legacy and continue to serve students. Critical to this work was the relationship between the two presidents.

I felt I was an (almost) equal partner with President Ali in this work. I drafted 25 versions of organizational charts, worked with each vice president at both RMUI and RU, and attended every open meeting I could get on the schedule. I needed to display positivity and forward momentum.

If You've Seen One Merger/Acquisition in Higher Education . . .

As the saying goes, "If you've seen one merger/acquisition in higher education, you've seen one merger/acquisition in higher education." Each one is quite different from another. Yet, we know this must be part of the fabric of higher education in the future to be able to scale a higher demand and level of services with a reduced number of students in the pipeline without pricing college out of their range. In addition, we know that the growth that will be possible in the Midwest will be with students who are more vulnerable and need greater assistance, delivered in more robust but different ways than in the past.

Although our missions were complementary, the schools' programming had only about a 40% overlap. Our student demographics had some similarities, but we also had many differences. Oh, and did I forget to mention that we were fierce athletic rivals? We had different calendars (quarter versus semester system) and faculty models (tenure-track vs. non-tenure-track), to name just a few. The teaching load, as an example, was night and day. Roosevelt has a typical three-course-a-semester tenured faculty teaching schedule, with non-tenure-track folks teaching four courses a semester. RMUI, with its focus on teaching and a quarter system, taught four courses a quarter, 15 in a calendar year. This was part of the value proposition. We knew these would be major hurdles to overcome, but the focus on mission and extending our legacies for the long term propelled us toward the integration.

The year 2018 was big for us. RMUI, as a commuter campus, did not have residence halls. However, about 200 of our student athletes desired an "on-campus" experience, resulting in us leasing space in private buildings throughout the city. In one of our friendly breakfast meetings, Ali mentioned RU had excess capacity in their beautiful residence halls half a block from our downtown location. What resulted was an agreement for 200 RMUI students to live in the residence halls of RU. Ali and I both saw this as a test of our ability to work together, beginning with negotiating the terms of this agreement. This didn't come easy, however. I recall a "deal-breaker" conversation when I demanded our students have an unlimited food option that previously had not been available. When it was met with resistance, I had to say, "Then we can't move forward." Okay, you're wondering why RMUI students needed more food? We had a football team, which was one of the groups that RU did not already have. Suffice it to say that our student athletes were treated exceptionally well, they could eat as much as they desired, and we were convinced we could do more together.

That year, we signed our first NDA and eventually an MOU. We set March 2020 as our goal to complete the transaction. Imperative in the planning was working with our regional accrediting body's timeline while moving ahead quickly so that our institutions were each as healthy as possible when we came together. Today, we see many universities beginning this work too late; it takes time and money. We met our goal of March 2020, but it wasn't easy.

A Few Invisible Yet Important Items

Words are important. From the very beginning, President Malekzadeh stressed that this was to be an integration of two cultures, not an assimilation. His own research expertise is in this area, which assisted with credibility to both universities' stakeholders. We intended to learn from each other and truly become a stronger university together.

Within the first few months of signing the NDA, each president began meeting with the other's board. Ali's first visit to the RMUI board lasted about ten minutes, with the goal of creating a level of comfort. The board learned of his background (his research interest is in the importance of culture in merger and acquisition in higher ed) and how he felt this relationship could extend the RMUI legacy. My visits with the Roosevelt board were centered on helping them see the value of our students, our faculty, and our professional staff, as well as how we could make Roosevelt University even better prepared to face the challenges of enrollment, finances, and social justice in the coming decades through our strategic fit. In retrospect, of course, it is easy to see that I was being evaluated personally by the board, the executive team, and the key stakeholders of Roosevelt University.

We planned a senior leadership retreat in the summer of 2019, after having 30-plus senior leaders sign NDAs. The leadership retreat was a day devoted to bringing our teams together. We brought in a consultant in higher education mergers and acquisitions to work with the teams. This day was instrumental in forming informal and formal connections, in helping our teams experience the camaraderie and working relationships the two presidents had already established, and in working through some natural anxiety. We ended the day with a bowling event, at which we discovered none of us would be joining the PBA circuit anytime soon.

We announced publicly our intent on October 2, 2019, adhering to the timeline of our accrediting body. It was week two of RMUI's fall quarter. Every minute of that day and the following few was tightly scheduled while also allowing for a few unplanned meetings. We met with faculty, staff, students, alumni, key donors, and athletic coaches (yes, they demanded their own impromptu meeting), and held town halls on that day. RU hosted a reception for faculty and staff the following day. Again, being about 250 steps door-to-door was extremely beneficial.

I cannot explain the sense of relief I felt when driving home late the evening of announcement day. Finally, I was able to talk about something that I believed strongly in and had been working tirelessly toward for years. I knew this was the right decision, at the right time, with the right university; that was my mantra during the "secret time." While I was beginning to feel a bit less anxious, this began the most challenging time for our faculty, staff, and students: the "Linus when his blanket is in the dryer" scenario.

> It's not so much that we're afraid of change or so in love with the old ways, but it's that place in between that we fear. . . . It's like being between trapezes. It's Linus when his blanket is in the dryer. There's nothing to hold on to.[1]

As soon as we announced our plans, I became exceedingly popular with other presidents. I had breakfast, lunch, and dinner invitations, and speaking engagements, all with the request to tell them how I made this happen. Particular interest centered on the entity being acquired. How did we make that decision? How did I get the board to agree?

Fast forward to March 9, the "wedding day." Roosevelt University had, in the prior six months, built out appropriate space for our students, faculty, and staff. We had begun relocating our community during the prior month, since we resided so closely to each other. Roosevelt University held open houses, conducted tours, and had welcome receptions. On March 10, President Ali and I spoke to more than 250 guests at a City Club luncheon in Chicago regarding the integration, further proof that people wanted to hear about how we made this happen. Little did we know that a week later we would all be working remotely for the next 12 to 18 months. Our integration happened at exactly the right time to utilize our combined strengths in infrastructure, IT, and personnel to assist our students in navigating the pandemic in the best way possible.

Secrets to a Successful Integration

It starts and ends with mission and culture. Ali's background in the culture of mergers and acquisitions was indispensable. We called it an "integration" to highlight our desire to bring out the best practices from each university. We intentionally illustrated examples. Early on, we created more than 35 task forces on assorted topics, with membership from both universities. In an initial call for volunteers, more than 240 responses (out of about 600 total employees) were received. Approximately 170 active task force members met biweekly; some still meet today. We reaped enormous benefits from this work. Our folks were already collaborating prior to the integration's official date. They recommended future practices while creating respect and camaraderie that would be needed when they became coworkers.

Behind the scenes, of course, work was being done to determine the legal structure of "The New Deal," as this integration was labeled.

Money was spent, attorneys were hired, and more money was spent. When it was determined that an acquisition was the best framework, a valuation of RMUI was completed. More money was spent; more attorneys were hired. We made daily decisions on IT systems, organization charts, academic programming, and even office locations. I also needed to determine, after the integration date, how I would "wind down" the RMUI operations while planning to be a member of the Roosevelt University community myself.

One of the most frequent questions I receive is, "What consultant did you use?" Quite frankly, we didn't. Over the years, I have utilized the expertise of many consultants, as had Roosevelt University. However, for this transaction, we knew what we wanted, we knew it was the right thing at the right time, and we decided to use consultants for specified reasons but not to guide the integration overall.

Ali and I met face-to-face semiweekly in our offices. This helped our community see us walking around together, meeting people, laughing, and getting along. We also instituted a 7 p.m. nightly phone call so that we were sure not to surprise one another. Things were moving forward at a breathtaking pace.

Lessons Learned

We had positive surprises. Students were supportive and trusted us to make the right and good decisions for them. Although we hosted multiple open meetings, students did not widely participate and were not overly concerned. A high anxiety level among faculty and staff was expected, and it was obvious. However, it was natural anxiety about change. Folks were overall extremely supportive and understood the need to be part of a larger entity in order to create choice and economies of scale. This did not come naturally. I had spent the past four years as president and many years as provost prior to this discussing the current environment of higher education, the Midwest's demographics, the students who deserved an RMUI education, and the legacy of our university.

The employees at Robert Morris knew this was an acquisition, so many fears about salaries, job security, and benefits were openly shared. I was surprised to see the anxiety felt by the Roosevelt University faculty and staff. They, too, knew of the need to do things differently. However, I had not thought about the natural fear of change on the part of the acquirer. What were they afraid of? That we were not as good as they? That we were better than they? Change in general?

I learned that some folks step up when you do not expect it, and others need to step out when they cannot accept change. I did make employment decisions during the month prior to the official date of acquisition. After hours of due diligence, I determined what positions I felt were not needed in the larger university and made those decisions accordingly. Sadly, while we were able to bring 35 full-time faculty and more than 100 staff members to Roosevelt University, I also made the difficult decision to not recommend offering positions to about 40 personnel. Until the last day as an independent university, RMUI decisions were made by me. Keeping an eye on the shared vision and the future made these tough decisions possible.

What Stands in the Way?

This work is *painful*. It is so difficult that unless both universities are experiencing a resounding need to move forward, obstacles can and will get in the way. For RMUI, it was long-term health. I knew the cost of leasing space in the city of Chicago would increase, that we needed to be in the city to serve our students, and that those very students could not bear the increased cost. I also desired to give our students more academic options. Roosevelt University had about a decade to determine how to best position themselves for long-term financial success, with a growing endowment, available space, and the need to expand programming to appeal to a larger number of urban students.

Sometimes the items that get in the way are not what you may expect. Culture trumps everything. At RMUI, our faculty had very nice individual space, but they were in a large room with cubicles. Roosevelt has a culture of offices; everyone has one. Many, many conversations were held about the number of offices needed when we did not need them. Would it be nice? Sure. But it was not necessary. All faculty now have offices . . . and I am happy for them.

Our work with alumni was quite pleasant. We informed our alumni of the impending change, assuring them that this meant greater networking capabilities and options for additional degrees for them. Roosevelt also held alumni events immediately after the public announcement, before our accrediting body approved the change of control. Alumni were welcomed and treated with respect. We also began to get them involved even prior to the official date. One of our RMUI alums is the mayor of Aurora, the second largest city in Illinois; he immediately agreed to speak on an alumni panel on a social justice topic. It was extremely well received.

Egos can get in the way. We all have them, and presidents of universities may have a larger than average opinion of themselves. Talking with the board, faculty, staff, students, and alumni about essentially changing the identity of your university is difficult. It can be seen as a failure if not communicated consistently and clearly. Egos of presidents and boards can and do get in the way of making needed changes. Being transparent about demographic changes in our geographic area, challenges for our universities, and shared strengths was key. We navigated through this challenge because of the foundation of trust built over the previous few years (and I knew we were being acquired). Beginning and ending every conversation with a discussion about students and mission was imperative. Trust, confidence, and chemistry on the part of both presidents was fundamental. It also meant I needed to trust in myself that I would figure out my own future, if that was needed.

Let's talk about athletics. One of the critical elements of this merger was number and type of student athletes. While we both competed at the same level (NAIA) and in the same conference (CCAC), RMUI had about three times the number of athletes as Roosevelt. We had football, cheer, dance, men's and women's hockey, men's and women's bowling, and esports to add to the RU structure. All teams were brought over with the head coaches intact for the added teams. The teams that were already in place at Roosevelt University, though, were met with skepticism on both sides. Our head coaches of those teams all became assistants, and in some respects, students were treated as second best. I recall a meeting with students when the men's basketball team of Roosevelt walked out, upset that we would be adding other students to the roster. Interestingly, however, almost three years later, the coaches who were the most upset are no longer in place. Many of the former RMUI head coaches (RU assistants) are now in the head coaching seats.

Three Years Later (But Who's Counting?)

The first year resulted in financial success for the university; our CFO's office tracked net revenue from students who came over from the former institution. A net gain of middle seven figures was attained within 12 months' time. Added to that were millions of federal dollars for those students from pandemic relief, which of course was not planned. Did I forget to mention the modality shift because of the pandemic slammed into us a week after the official date of the integration? We were able to immediately share costs across more students in areas such as facilities, institutional memberships, software, and expertise.

Our IT conversion went faster than expected. Our calendar change from quarters to semesters was completed on an accelerated timeline at the demands of our staff in those areas. The university used a website, "Building a Stronger University," to communicate updates on a weekly and sometimes daily basis. Our retention did go down by about 3% during the first year. While we are diagnosing what those students may have had in common, we also know that correlation may not mean causation. Was it the integration that complicated their plans? Was it the pandemic? Was it the unrest in the city of Chicago?

The bottom line is that it was a financial success immediately. Long term will depend, of course, on our continuing to leverage our strengths as a combined entity. We now have expanded programs in health care because of the integration, which was instrumental in creating a new

College of Science, Health, and Pharmacy. We dramatically expanded our student athlete opportunities. We are beginning to plan new programs based around our collective faculty and staff.

RU now has a discount model that is remarkably similar to what we had at RMUI, allowing students with greater financial need the option of attending Roosevelt. We also have greater contacts with the public school systems, a legacy of RMUI relationships. It has been fun to see the trajectory of some of our faculty and staff. One of our faculty was elected to one of five faculty trustee positions within the first six months. Our CFO is the former CFO of RMUI; one of our associate deans is a former RMUI faculty member. I was given the opportunity to be the interim provost for a year, a position I never expected to fill since I do not come from the tenure-track ranks of faculty. I was also asked to chair our Strategic Planning Steering Committee, which consisted of faculty, administrators, students, and board members. We completed the work in a semester, and it was unanimously approved by the board of trustees.

Of course, an acquisition is not two equals coming together. A tough reminder has been that when folks do not like an answer or see a problem, the acquired entity might get some blame. Retention is down? It must be those RMUI students. Health care costs went up? It must be those RMUI employees. We need a new manager in a certain area? We need to hire from outside. This is human nature, yet a stark reminder that this was not the merger of two equals. Over the first few years, some fundamental differences have become more glaring. Our faculty structure is one example. While Roosevelt University did have some full-time non-tenure-track faculty, about 75% were tenured or tenure-track. Many policies are still in place that allow only tenured faculty to hold positions on councils, boards, and in leadership positions. This is not mentioned as a criticism necessarily; however, those policies do not reflect the current demographics of the faculty. To a certain extent, it may be causing tenured folks to hold on tighter and resist change.

What could have gone better? Of course, room for improvement always exists. Different, while not wrong, is different. As president of RMUI, as it became obvious that some practices, products, or people were not appreciated, I needed to prioritize. We did lose some relation-ships, people, and programs in areas that we are now trying to rebuild. I see this as a natural outcome, but I could have worked harder to preserve institutional knowledge. Let me be clear; people were re-spected as individuals but not necessarily as equals in terms of knowl-edge or aptitude. People, organizations, and relationships are constantly changing, regardless of the merger/acquisition, and regardless of the pandemic. We did have a debrief session with the Executive Committee related to what we have learned. I believe we could have dug in a bit more, especially since we see acquisition work as a central piece of our strategic plan.

As a former president, I needed to navigate not being "the one" at my new institution. Although I was a reluctant president early on, I grew to genuinely enjoy the position and unintentionally became comfort-able with being the person others turned to for the final decision. I re-spect hierarchy, and I take direction very well. However, admittedly, I still give myself a daily reminder that I am *not* at the top of the organizational chart at Roosevelt. A few months ago, a colleague said to me, "You still think like a president!" I'm not sure that was meant as a compliment. Some days not being at the top is a relief; other times, it is a challenge.

Summary

Mergers and acquisitions in higher education can and do work. It be-gins with finding commonality or complementarity in missions and strategic plans. We were similar but not identical. We had early "wins" with key leaders. We entered into the housing agreement for our student athletes as a pilot, and it worked. We became constant communicators. We included 30-plus leaders in an NDA, and they *honored it*! And, yes, we were half a block from each other.

Did we disagree? Of course. However, our trusting relationship, built over time, allowed us to work through those disagreements. I recall one of our two days of negotiation with attorneys in the room. We were each getting advice from attorneys to stand strong. Ali and I decided to send the attorneys out of the room so that we could make progress on our own. We knew this was what was needed, we knew our universities best, and we knew we had each other's trust.

Would we do it again? This particular one, of course; it worked. Others? Sure. Which ones? It depends. What we know is that collaborations and partnerships *must be* considered in the future for higher education and certainly for Roosevelt University. We have other alliances already with shared space and shared programming in the works. We know we have a strong infrastructure that we can leverage across more students. We know we have talented individuals who run this infrastructure. The most challenging time is when Linus's blanket is in the dryer, but at the end you have a clean, fresh, warm blanket. Roosevelt University sees this work as not simply one transaction but as a central piece of its strategic plan and model for the future.

Presidents *must* be cheerleaders! They must each be seen as a team captain, be constant communicators, become relentless in their belief in the transaction, and highlight early wins. Finding cause for celebration, including all stakeholders, is extremely important. Three years later, one of the fond memories we have is a reception following the announcement, which brought together our faculty and staff. The Roosevelt University folks during that two hours were instrumental in welcoming their new colleagues.

I look forward to continuing to be employable and employed in higher education, regardless of what my friend shared with me. (Yes, he is still my friend.) I have learned a lot, and I want the chance to use it to assist more students in the future. Identifying the right partners, combined with impeccable planning and execution, can create positive change for the universities but, more important, for the students we serve. I believe without a doubt that the best outcome for the RMUI students in 2020 was to assist them in becoming graduates of Roosevelt University.

Note

1. "Marilyn Ferguson Quotes." Goodreads, www.goodreads.com/author/quotes/207146 .Marilyn_Ferguson.

CHAPTER SIX

How a Failed Merger Attempt Helped Create the Conditions for Success

PAUL J. MAURER
President, Montreat College

THE STORY OF THIS chapter revolves around the idea *that a failed merger attempt may help create the conditions for success* for a college. Failure to merge may be a tremendous step in the *right* direction. Sometimes an upward trajectory begins after hitting rock bottom. That's the story of Montreat College.

Founded in 1916 by a group of devout Presbyterians just outside Asheville, North Carolina, Montreat College has educated students for more than a century. It has served Appalachia and the Southeast, preparing educators, nonprofit and business leaders, and medical professionals for lives of service. Montreat College has always had a small enrollment, with a main campus built of stone for 500 students against a picturesque mountain cove. Being small has its pros and cons. On the positive side, the education is personal, and students get to be a big fish in a small pond. On the negative side, financial resources for small schools are often a challenge.

Given the written and verbal history of Montreat College, it seems clear that most of its existence has been lived in economic survival mode. While educating students year after year for the common good, the college seems to have always struggled to have enough money. The college has never been wealthy, highly selective, or possessed a large endowment. Being in survival mode creates a culture of scarcity, which makes it hard to envision a growing, healthy, or prosperous future. A culture of scarcity defaults to what can be cut, not added. It also creates an environment that is risk-averse, because it feels like there is no room for error. If you are unfamiliar with private higher education in the United States, there are perhaps hundreds of colleges and universities that fit this profile. These institutions dot the landscape in both rural and urban settings, with faculty and staff who teach and serve because they believe deeply in the mission of the college. The employees are not principally motivated by money but rather by the chance to influence the intellectual and social development of the next generation of students. Some are faith-based, others are not.

Today, Montreat College is financially healthier than at any time in decades, perhaps more so than any time in its history. Just a few years ago, in 2014, the college was on the brink of closure, following a failed attempt at merger. The attempted merger was, like so many others, a situation of desperation. Enrollment had dropped steeply over several years and the basic business model of the college was failing and getting worse. In 2012, 29 full-time employees were laid off. Despite repeated cuts and an extremely thin budget, annual operational revenue was far below expenses. With residential undergrad enrollment fewer than 400 students, it certainly seemed unsustainable. Nevertheless, the adage "It's hard to kill a college" applied to Montreat College. Year after year, an extraordinary group of donors who believed in the mission of the college would give, keeping the doors open.

Merger Exploration

By 2012, with a choking operational deficit, a merger was beginning to be seen by many on the college's board of trustees as the best, and perhaps only, future for the college. This was not an entirely new thought. Over the years, Montreat had reached out to colleges in our region to inquire about merger, but none of these conversations gained traction. In January 2013, a meaningful conversation began with Point University in Georgia, about a five-hour drive away. Although a completely unrelated event, that same month the college's payroll and benefits director was arrested for embezzling more than $250,000 from the college, and a month later pleaded guilty to ten felonies and was sentenced to state prison. This only added to the sense of instability.

The college entered an NDA with Point and began a lengthy negotiation. When the merger exploration was announced in the summer of 2013, it was quickly and deeply unpopular among some of Montreat's alumni. As the summer turned to fall, the complications of merger became increasingly clear, including some tricky property challenges and the fear that the merger would shutter Montreat's main residential campus. The faculty rose in opposition. By the end of 2013 and in early 2014, anger had grown, protests were held, and the faculty took a vote of no confidence in the board, calling on all who favored the merger to resign. Press coverage of the growing controversy intensified the situation.

Even though both institutions worked hard to develop a partnership that would be mutually beneficial, it did not work out as hoped. Therefore, Point's board voted to discontinue the merger consideration in February 2014. Ultimately, there was no one to blame. The complications of this proposed merger were too much.

This left Montreat College in a weaker and more precarious situation than ever. With trust severely degraded, the year of merger exploration had further eroded the college as employees, including senior leaders, left for greener pastures, and organizational charts were redrawn in anticipation of the merger. Several positions became vacant, and these were much harder to fill given the circumstances. Basic operations, such as mowing the college's soccer field, fell through the cracks. The vote of no confidence in the board of trustees, along with searing alumni criticism, led several fine trustees to leave the board. A general toxicity, rooted in hopelessness, malaise, and distrust, had fallen over the college.

Montreat College hit rock bottom. It now faced a near-death experience. As a faith-based college, there seemed to be only two options: (1) close its doors or (2) have God show up in a big way.

During the merger conversation, one of the college's adjunct faculty members took the initiative to reach out to a most unique couple. The faculty member is the pastor of a local church about 30 minutes from campus. He has taught at the college for years and is a great champion of how the college seeks to educate and prepare the next generation of leaders. About 18 months before Montreat's near-death experience, this couple from another state visited beautiful Western North Carolina for a seven-month sabbatical with their homeschooled children. During this time, the couple and their children occasionally attended his church. But the church is large enough that you can remain anonymous if you choose to. The couple and their children came and went without him knowing who they were.

After their sabbatical, the couple returned to their home. But the work of the church lingered with them. They were impressed with the church's commitment to the poor, located in one of the poorest counties in North Carolina. They reached out to inquire how they could help. The pastor's response was vague. They responded by sending a very generous check to support the church's effort. And then they sent another check. And another.

With Montreat College in a bad place, he chose to take a risk. Knowing it could undermine the couple's giving to his church, he inquired whether the couple might consider supporting Montreat College and its now rare mission of educating students with a deep commitment to faith-based education.

The couple had no connection to the college. They are not alumni, had never stepped foot on campus, and had never spoken with anyone from the college. At that point, Montreat College was simply the name of a college they knew nothing about. This pastor was their sole point of contact. When they expressed an openness to learn more, the pastor reached out to the college. Understandably, the college wanted to meet the couple in person, or at least speak by phone. Well, at least know their names. It was reasonable to want to know these were real human beings, and that they had financial resources. But none of that was going to happen. Ultimately, the couple trusted him, and they wanted him to remain their sole emissary.

After the merger discussions formally ended, the discussion with this couple continued over the next few weeks. The board of trustees and the couple went back and forth with more information and numbers. The pastor remained in the middle, hoping and praying the couple would make a gift large enough to give the college a chance to survive. On March 1, 2014, the couple pledged $6 million to the college. It would be unrestricted. And it would be anonymous. Through a foundation, they would begin to send $300,000 a month to the church, who would in turn route it to the college's bank account. The gifts began right away.

In our faith community, we believe a miracle is something only God can do. The sudden, out-of-context, and random nature of the anonymous couple's gift was stunning. It was also a clear signal to the college community that God was not finished with Montreat College. To this day, our community sees this as a miracle, and we retell the story often. We tell it over and over for at least two reasons. The first is that we never want to lose perspective on who is ultimately responsible for all the good news of recent years. Yes, the donor gave the money. But they have often said that they acted in obedience and faith that they were supposed to give that money to the college. *They* see God as ultimately the one to whom the glory goes. We do too.

The second reason we retell the story is that my job, our job, is to steward a miracle. That is different than simply rebuilding a college. We have been given a great opportunity, and with this comes tremendous responsibility. I've learned the purpose of the miracle: it's to point to God so he gets the glory. I've also learned what miracles are not: they are not a ticket to easy street. The purpose of a miracle is not to make life easy, or even easier. The years that followed made that abundantly clear.

What Part of "No" Don't You Understand?

A few weeks after the miracle pledge, I was approached to be a candidate for president. Not interested. After two lengthy conversations with

Bill Peterson, the search firm executive, my wife, Joellen, and I agreed that we were *definitely* not interested. Frankly, I did not want "closed Montreat College" on my CV. Bill asked if I'd be willing to come to North Carolina for "just one conversation" with the search committee. That seemed harmless enough. Sensing no danger of becoming interested, it would be good experience. When I arrived on Tuesday for my "conversation," I learned I had been named a finalist, despite not submitting any application material. By the end of the week, the search committee was ready to make an offer. I was not only reluctant, but resistant. In the days that followed, Joellen wondered whether this might be God's way of calling us to a new season.

There were a lot of hard questions. I wanted to meet the anonymous couple to understand their long-term commitment. I was told I would meet them if I became president. Strike one. I reviewed lots of financial data. Even with the anonymous couple, things did not look good. Although $6 million is a lot of money, it was clear it would not solve the college's annual multimillion-dollar business model problem. Strike two.

But not all the news was bad. In fact, there was significant good news. The pledge by the anonymous couple, while not solving the operating revenue problem, provided a bridge and could be used as leverage toward a new reality. In fact, it *had* to be leveraged to create increased annual revenue, and not simply spent on operations, because otherwise the college would spend all $6 million and never really move the needle away from unsustainability. It was also evidence that God and was not finished with Montreat College, which provided a powerful and fresh hope for the future. The board was made up of quality people who loved the college, and despite the drama of the past year, they remained unified in crucial ways. There was a group of loyal and committed donors who were very generous to the college. As important as anything, I began to understand the employees, and perhaps especially the faculty, had a palpable desire for a future, especially for a vibrant residential undergraduate program.

Over the following days, we sought the counsel of family and close friends, deliberated, and prayed for guidance. Against our rational human judgment, we began to experience a sense of call. Once we decided this was what we were supposed to do, we were all in. We joined a group of alumni, trustees, and supporters in the All In campaign they launched as a tangible means of claiming a future for the college.

"Change or Die" Becomes "Change Fast or Die"

I remember well the early months of my first presidency, beginning in January 2009. The Great Recession, which began in October 2008, was wreaking havoc in the broader economy, and higher education was not spared. Within five weeks of my start date, I announced layoffs and budget cuts. To their credit, no one at my institution blamed the new guy, because it was clear to everyone that layoffs and cuts were happening everywhere. I went to two or three presidents' conferences to begin to get my bearings. I came back to campus with a summary of what I had heard: "Change or die." It was a sobering way to begin. But the message could not have been clearer.

Higher education is not only slow to change but often adverse to it. After all, very smart people have created thousands of institutions of higher learning that have successfully spawned the greatest middle class in the history of the world. Traditions are strong. People tend to be set in their ways. And most people prefer change that does not affect them. Thus, being a champion of change in higher education is a risky venture. Many presidents are afraid to change things "too much" for fear they'll receive the dreaded, and mostly misguided, "vote of no confidence" from the faculty and subsequently lose their job.

By the time I began my tenure at Montreat in 2014, I sensed the narrative at presidents' conferences had changed a bit since 2009. In my hearing, they added the word *fast*. The new mantra was "change *fast* or die."

President as Chief Executive Officer (CEO) and Chief Urgency Officer (CUO)

In many higher education settings, the president needs to function not only as president but also as CEO. Some may see these roles as synonymous, but there's a nuanced difference. Being a CEO means executive decisions are made, and that responsibility for those decisions ultimately rests in one place. Shared governance in higher education means different things in different places. I subscribe to a version where faculty should own the curriculum and have input in other academic decisions and in the formation of academic matters in the strategic plan, but little more. This means the president, with deliberation, agreement, and buy-in from the executive leadership team, makes the daily operational decisions for the institution.

However, in this season of disruption in higher education, the president as CEO is not enough. The president also needs to be chief urgency officer (CUO). Establishing a sense of urgency is the first of John Kotter's change principles in his outstanding book *Leading Change*. Kotter says, "By far the biggest mistake people make when trying to change organizations is to plunge ahead without establishing a high enough sense of urgency in fellow managers and employees. This error is fatal because transformations always fail to achieve their objective when complacency levels are high."[1] He continues, "Without a sense of urgency, people won't give that extra effort that is often essential. They won't make the needed sacrifices. Instead, they cling to the status quo and resist initiatives from above."[2]

In the same way only the president can be the CEO, if the president does not wear the mantle of CUO, no one will. Today's higher ed environment requires a constant sense of urgency from the president. Having a president who owns the roles of both CEO and CUO may mean the difference between an institution that persistently struggles with one that is financially healthy. It may also be the difference between the life and death of an institution.

The Elements That Created Openness to Major Change

Kotter's *Leading Change* was a guidebook for me, and over time I came to value its insights and practical usefulness even more deeply. Without needing to articulate each of the principles here, it provided a means to develop my own narrative for our community. It was important to talk about change at all our monthly all-employee meetings, as well as at monthly faculty meetings. It went something like this: "We have a vision and a promising future guided by a plan, but it requires building or rebuilding most elements of our college. Our basic business model is badly broken. We must grow enrollment, fix our dysfunctional systems, and be creative and innovative. It will take an extraordinary commitment from each of us. And we must hurry." The message was essentially the same every month for years. It was packaged a bit differently each month and included every scrap of good news of our progress.

We also faced the reality that the college had received a lot of bad press coverage and anyone who paid attention to us over time considered us weak and living on the brink of failure. The impact of the failed merger only deepened the negative image of the college. Add to that the distrust and lack of confidence some of our alumni had toward not only the board of trustees but anyone in administrative leadership at the college. This distrust extended to the new president despite repeated attempts to encourage them to join the effort to create a new and exciting future.

The most important *initial* factor to open our community to major change was the failed merger. But it alone does not explain the full picture. There were a handful of other essential elements, some drawn directly from Kotter, that helped to root the idea of change as a long-term cultural reality.

Mission and Vision

As a mission-centric college, most of our employees are motivated by our mission and animated by our long-term vision. Having a vision means we must work together to achieve a different reality, and that it takes everyone to get there. We carefully screen job applicants for mission and vision, and it creates an institutional unity and culture that is powerful. We have a pretty good idea why our people come to work in the morning.

Core Values

We narrate a set of values that supersede the daily tasks of our work. We openly prioritize personal humility, the development of trust with each other, and that relationships matter more than getting the job done. Effectiveness done with excellence is extremely important, but it's number four after humility, trust, and relationships. The final three core values are: a sense of urgency, belief that God is at work among us, and extraordinary commitment. Lived out, even though imperfectly, it signals to our community that goals, excellence, progress, and achievement can be expected in a healthy work and relationship culture.

The Board of Trustees

There was a remarkable level of situational and self-awareness by the board. They helped create the culture of change by humbly modeling it. That awareness led some to step off the board, recognizing the experience of the failed merger had left them bruised or burned out. For those who remained, they recognized the need to reconsider how the board conducted its business, which led to the adoption of the new board policy manual. Finally, they knew we needed to aggressively recruit new trustees. We developed a rich and exciting plan and they gave me the green light to lead the process.

Transparency about the Difficult Road Ahead

It seemed important to make sure our employees understood we had a long, steep climb ahead of us. Years, not months. They heard it regularly. And while they did not always hear the details of the worst challenges, they consistently heard about the need to persevere for the long term. Transparency builds trust.

The Power of Small Wins

We learned the power of small wins and looked for regular and tangible ways to create and report good news. It was surprising how powerful a regular *drip-drip* of small wins was for our campus culture. Ironically, steady small wins were made easier because we had so much deferred maintenance. Donor support was growing steadily as the good news slowly replaced the bad and we did several mini campaigns. We made a big deal when we renovated the fitness center, created a black box theater, and opened a cybersecurity teaching lab. We constantly asked donors to fund opportunities to take another step in the right direction. We tried to do three to five physical upgrades each year in addition to new programs or other tangible progress. Nothing was too small to celebrate. Every six months, we continue to send a progress update to all our constituents.

Setbacks and Momentum

We've had setbacks, such as being put on warning for a year for financial weakness after our decennial accreditation visit. We also had a wealthy prospective donor who made multiple promises about funding major projects whose promises turned out to be empty. Some initiatives have not worked, such as trying to establish a recruitment pipeline from China. But we've also experienced authentic momentum, which motivates people to keep pressing toward the vision. Momentum must be communicated regularly for it to be part of the culture. It is the rising tide that lifts all boats, even when you must work extra hard to convince some that their boat is also rising.

We Cannot Cut Our Way to Health: Growth through a Promise, New Academic Programs and Other Pipelines, and Becoming Externally Facing

We had to *grow* our way to health, because we knew we could not *cut* our way to health. There was no fat to cut. Enrollment growth was imperative. Without it, there was no possibility of fixing the business model. We knew we had to hustle because the clock was ticking. The anonymous donors' pledge would be fulfilled in about two years, and we had to generate more annual operational revenue to have a chance to succeed. It also meant *increasing* annual expenditures because we had to invest in programs we believed would generate future revenue, knowing there would be a gap in time between the investment and the return.

There was no room for wishful thinking. A miracle is not magic and does not erase long-standing systemic problems. We had to think, plan, be data-driven, and have extraordinary commitment to the road ahead.

We had to execute. The gift from the anonymous donor needed to be used for leverage. It also needed to be catalytic.

A Promise

The very first thing we did was to take a major step to clarify our institutional identity, which had gotten blurry in the previous years. We wanted to be crystal clear about who we are. We embraced the notion that no college or university is for everyone. Virtually every university, large or small, draws mostly from a regional geography and appeals to a particular kind of student. As such, we crafted a crisp and clear promise to the marketplace of prospective students and their parents, cognizant and comfortable that we were defining a niche. We understood that there were only a few remaining faith-based institutions within our main geographic reach, and so our promise was a combination of who we are and the recognition that we could position ourselves to compete favorably for a certain segment of the market. The promise goes like this:

> Montreat College is an independent, Christ-centered, liberal arts college that educates students through intellectual inquiry, spiritual formation, and preparation for calling and career.

One of the great advantages of being small is the opportunity to be agile. No red tape or endless committee meetings. Important decisions can be made quickly. Within a few weeks we had buy-in from the faculty and other key stakeholders. We quickly went to print, created short videos, and started organizing "Meet Montreat" events in cities within 250 miles of campus. We assumed we would have to go find students rather than them finding us. We called this our "road show." Over several years, we executed more than 60 Meet Montreat gatherings, and the central message of each event was to unpack our clarified identity. We had two target audiences. The first was influencers who speak into the college decision process, such as high school guidance counselors, youth leaders, and pastors. This helped us to build a network of influencers who saw us in a fresh light and put us on their radar. The second target audience was prospective students and their parents. These events were well attended, and we decided to do more events for as long as we believed they were strategic and effective.

New Academic Programs

I had heard for years about the need for small colleges to establish an academic niche, something they are known for. Our faith identity was not enough. Historically, we were known for our outdoor education program. We still were, but it had modest prospects for growth. State, regional, and national job growth projections largely revolve around STEM-related fields, so with faculty agreement, we decided to focus most of our growth investment toward STEM. We started with technology.

My first year at Montreat was our first year with a BS in cybersecurity. With no previous knowledge about cybersecurity, I noticed stories about it on the front page of the *New York Times* several days a week. Thinking we had an opportunity for something big, we decided to swing for the fences. We went all in to build the program, believing we could add a substantial number of students and help shape a new brand. We hired a lobbyist on the theory that we could scale the program through a public–private partnership. Together, we began to visit Washington, DC, about every 60 days to test a value proposition and build relationships. After testing a value proposition for a year in numerous meetings, we gained the confidence to settle on one that is unique in the market of cybersecurity programs.

We also invested in growing our nascent honors program, which we built as a "great books, big questions" program focused on classic readings in the liberal arts. The honors program is delivered through the general ed curriculum, which provides the ability for students to participate in the program regardless of their major. Both cybersecurity and honors also gave us ways to recruit stronger academic students, which was central to our vision. In all, we picked five academic areas for growth. To their credit, the faculty agreed with the need to focus our investment and growth in a few areas in the strategic plan.

New Athletic Programs

Although we continue to have an imbalance between the percentage of athletes and nonathletes, we nonetheless also added several new athletic programs. Fixing the balance would have to come later. We needed to build reliable enrollment pipelines.

Unapologetically Market-Driven

Looking back after almost 25 years in higher ed administration, my experience is that colleges are not especially externally facing, and at times they can be quite insular. Insularity is the corollary to resistance to change. For us, becoming externally facing was not only about recruitment events in our region. It is more fundamentally tied to having our academic programs and curriculum in alignment with what the market wants. New programs are considered only if they have significant potential for growth according to market research analysis.

Turnaround Becomes Start-Up

For about two years, I used the language and concepts of a turnaround. Constantly, perhaps a bit relentlessly. Then, I had a paradigm-shifting aha moment. It's one of those moments you remember clearly. I was in my office, meeting with a local start-up entrepreneur. He was describing what he was trying to do, but more importantly, he was describing *how* he was doing it. I am not sure he intended to outline the guiding principles for a start-up, but that is what I heard: agility, creativity, fast decision-making, fail quickly, take risks, starve what does not work and feed what does. I asked him if there was a key book that I could read to begin to understand start-up thinking. He recommended Eric Ries's *The Lean Startup*. He said it was central to the canon of start-up books. Between that conversion and the book, I was not only energized but began to think that our work was more of a start-up than a turnaround.

But I needed to verify that before I could consider changing my narrative. So I asked our longest-serving faculty member. I explained the new paradigm I was considering, suggesting that a turnaround implied a return to some former glory. "Was there a time when the college was financially strong and healthy?" He responded, "In my 40-plus years at Montreat, we have always been in survival mode." He understood the big-picture nature of my question and I had my answer. And although I continued to test the narrative with other long-termers, I began to proclaim, "We are a 100-year-old start-up!"

The start-up narrative is more than a talking point. If it is going to mean anything, it must change the way we think and act. I began to read a series of business books about start-up principles, leaders, and success stories. And I began to meet with successful start-up entrepreneurs to hear their experience and advice of how they thought I should apply the principles to higher ed. I spent more and more time with these people. These readings and conversations led me to think more about being a start-up leader. Thinking more about being a start-up leader led me into new kinds of conversations with my cabinet and board. And of course, all this naturally led to decisions that reflected start-up thinking and principles.

The effect of all this created tremendous energy. Within me. Within my cabinet. Within my board. Within many employees. Within donors and prospective donors, especially business leaders who think higher ed is weird and largely inept at knowing how to make itself sustainable. To be sure, there were skeptics. But no one tried to derail this new part of our identity and trajectory, and over time we achieved critical mass with key stakeholders. Now, several years in, being a start-up is central to our identity and has helped redefine the college.

Fresh Energy with Fresh Personnel

Many of the personnel who labored at Montreat College during decades of financial uncertainty, or worse, on the brink of financial exigency, have something of a heroic quality to them. They served because they believed deeply in the mission, and they served with tremendous commitment and loyalty. However, mergers take a toll on personnel. As our merger exploration continued for an entire year, ultimately ending without a success, some personnel chose to leave, making decisions in the best interests of their families.

Others chose to stay. For those who stayed, I would put them into two categories: (1) those who had some grasp of the need for the future of college to look very different from the past and (2) those who did not. The easiest adjustment was for those who grasped the need for change. For some, a sort of "merger trauma" meant it was best for them to step away.

Change in personnel is normal, necessary, and challenging, and is an opportunity. When I began, I had five open cabinet positions. It made my first year particularly challenging. But I also knew I could quickly establish my own team, something every president needs to do. Sooner is better. As my cabinet and other new employees came aboard, fresh energy embraced the fresh vision.

A New Revenue Source

Given the broken business model of our college, we attempted to create a significant new revenue stream to supplement our traditional revenue streams. We believed it needed to be big. In our version, we pursue cybersecurity. We have two objectives: (1) to serve the common good by hardening the cybersecurity defenses of the businesses and municipalities of the state of North Carolina and (2) to monetize our cybersecurity expertise to create a significant revenue stream to support the growth of the college. As such, in 2020 we launched the Carolina Cyber Center as a project of the college. We pivoted our government relations efforts to focus on our elected state officials, who shared in our vision for a public–private partnership between academia, business, and government. They generously provided start-up funding and subsequently funded an ambitious plan to accelerate statewide workforce development in cybersecurity. So far, the Carolina Cyber Center is fulfilling its first objective to serve the common good but has not yet begun to fulfill the second. Ultimately, we don't know if that part of the vision will succeed. If not, we'll seek a different model to generate alternate revenue.

Today and Tomorrow

Montreat College has experienced multiple years of record high enrollment while lowering its discount rate, which is now below the national average for private institutions. This is evidence that the college has raised its value proposition in the marketplace, essential for a struggling institution. Cybersecurity is now our second largest major and honors has grown substantially. Combined, they are reshaping our academic culture in good and healthy ways. We added other programs, and they contribute to the overall trajectory toward financial health. The anonymous couple has given a total of nearly $11 million, all unrestricted. Their gifts were indeed catalytic, as they inspired other donors, old and new, to give generously. Their miracle gift also helped inspire our employees and trustees to believe that Montreat College has a God-given destiny. We are now growing our online degree offerings and have recently added 15 new undergraduate and master's programs, which we hope will grow substantially. The college is experiencing success in its first capital campaign in about 30 years. And while it took seven hard years to achieve an operational surplus, the team persevered and never lost hope. We have entered new territory for Montreat College: the beginnings of financial health. It's good, but it's just the beginning. We have a long way to go. It all started with a failed merger attempt.

Learning to Believe in Ourselves

Almost ten years into this now-108-year-old start-up, our community has begun to believe in themselves. Having experienced that transition at a former institution, I'm watching it create a powerful new dynamic on campus and with our publics. We have begun to see our future differently, and that has exciting implications.

Conclusion

If you're a leader in higher education, you know the need for meaningful change is real. At the risk of boiling it down too simplistically, there are two conditions that precede all others. The first is that presidents must lead the change. There is no one else. The second is that boards must support their presidents as they lead change, and they must not listen too closely to the inevitable cries of protest that come with it. I suggest that these two conditions are nonnegotiable. Beyond these, perhaps the Montreat College story illustrates other principles that could be considered as college leadership seeks to chart the pathway to a new future.

Notes
1. John P. Kotter. 2012. *Leading Change* (Cambridge, MA: Harvard Business Review Press), 4.
2. Kotter, *Leading Change*, 5.

CHAPTER SEVEN

Redefining Success

Creating Urgency and Changing Perceptions

—————

ROBERT E. CLARK II

President Emeritus, Wesley College

ON JULY 1, 2021, Wesley College became part of Delaware State University's downtown campus as the Wesley College of Health and Behavioral Sciences. This effort was a culmination of almost four years of a college and community trying tirelessly to ensure that an institution that had provided life-changing opportunities for students for almost 150 years, many of whom in the past several decades came from underserved communities, did not become a 55-acre plot of boarded-up buildings in downtown Dover, Delaware. Wesley College has been an institution that has evolved over its history, both in functionality and name, as it graduated young men and women of purpose for our community and region. Though the name and educational focus areas of this institution have changed over time, the life-changing educational opportunities provided to so many have remained the bedrock of what has made, and will continue to make, Wilmington Academy, Wesley Junior College, Wesley College, and now, hopefully, Delaware State University's Wesley College of Health and Behavioral Sciences a special place, and their alums leaders of positive change in the communities that they live in and serve.

The full scope of the impact of this acquisition, and the potential that it could have on increasing educational opportunities while also being part of a community revitalization effort, is far from being fully quantified. Wesley's story provides not only some broad insights into how this historic acquisition came to pass but most importantly, and hopefully, generates honest and focused discussions regarding the current state of higher education in our country—both in terms of the business model and pedagogy. What we faced at Wesley College is not a unique scenario. The rate of college closures continues to increase, and without all levels of the campus community having honest discussions about how they can best provide life-changing educational opportunities to the students and communities they serve, not only now, but more importantly in the future, the rate of closures will only increase. Having a clarity of reality of your institution's current relevance, as well as its future potential, is critical so that discussions can be had, and options mapped out, to ensure that when change comes you are ready with options—and not react to an inevitability of circumstances that could have been mitigated.

The Writing Is on the Wall . . . So Why Is It So Hard to Understand?

Face reality as it is, not as it was or as you wish it to be.

—JACK WELCH[1]

Arriving at Wesley College in the summer of 2015, it was apparent from day one that significant challenges faced the college. Discontinuities and "red flags" could be found in every aspect and area of the college, complacency was rampant, and pockets of divisiveness were present among the faculty. To understand why the discontinuities, complacency, and divisiveness existed, it was important to understand the contributing variables—externally as well as internally.

Wesley College is located in downtown Dover, Delaware, which, like many small cities across the country, has experienced a decline in its downtown district. Dover's challenges are reflective of those faced by Charleston, South Carolina, in the 1970s—empty storefronts, pockets of crime, vagrancy, and a visible socioeconomic divide. Similarly, the potential of transformation that Charleston realized to become such a vibrant and thriving destination city today is a potential that resides in Dover with the building blocks of a strong health care presence, a historic downtown district, and the potential of a revitalized college. Conscious of the current state of the surrounding area (an external variable), we always made it a priority to enact decisions regarding Wesley College with an understanding that they would also have a direct and positive impact on the community.

Dover is the state capital, and the Legislative Mall is only a few blocks from the campus, yet there was no sustained effort by the college to engage with local or, especially, state leadership for support and partnerships on a consistent or expansive basis. We were lacking in providing a concise and compelling argument for Wesley's Worth, let alone cultivating potential investors. It was important to flip the narrative from "giving money to a distressed college" to "investing in our collective future," and a concerted effort was made to spend several days a week at Legislative Hall engaging state leadership and their staffs.

Why, though, when tangible evidence of a college in dire straits was evident in many areas, was the writing on the wall so hard to understand? Or was it read and understood but not believed? Maybe it was understood but not acted upon because there was a sense that change could not occur without adequate resources, or there was an unwillingness to change. Yet impediments to change are not always simple or people related. As Chip and Dan Heath detail in their book, *Switch: How to Change Things When Change Is Hard*, "What looks like a people problem is often a situation problem."[2] The more we listened, and the more we learned, the more we became convinced that addressing the culture (situation) would be key to effecting change. We needed to take action to change the culture so our college, and community, could move forward. Replacing reactivity with proactivity, as well as replacing "personality-driven" with "process-driven," allowed us to build a culture of shared ownership, responsibility, and accountability. If we could change the culture and get the talent that resided in our collective Wesley College family (staff; faculty; students; alums; local, state, and federal leadership; business and foundation partnerships; and our community friends and neighbors) engaged, we could help mitigate, or change, some of the contributing variables that continued to negatively impact our campus and community.

Coming to the Decision That a Fundamental Change in the Business Model Was Needed

> Change is the law of life. Those who look only to the past or the present are certain to miss the future.
>
> —PRESIDENT JOHN F. KENNEDY[3]

By the fall of 2016, we had made a noticeable improvement in establishing a culture of shared ownership, responsibility, and accountability, which would be instrumental in helping move the college forward. Unfortunately, we continued to face significant financial and operational challenges.

We took a campus-wide "deep dive" to ensure we were addressing the many prevalent issues and shortfalls while also being open to finding others that needed to be addressed. One of the approaches used to get everyone thinking more proactively was the concept of picking an event, or issue, that had not yet occurred and then discussing the actions and needs that would have to be realized to mitigate the event/issue. This process would allow us to discuss potential future issues, such as operational efficiencies, infrastructure issues, financial burdens, public affairs plans, and potential staff/faculty/student/alumni concerns, as well as community problems, to name just a few. This type of "what if" and "then if, what/how?" way of proactive planning is an exercise that is commonly used by the United States Navy's Submarine Force to improve operational efficiency and effectiveness. There will always be time to critique, so why not take the time to think through and plan for potential events before they occur in order to give yourself a better chance of success?

Several years ago, during my time as the Commandant of Midshipmen at the United States Naval Academy, Guy Kawasaki gave me a copy of his book *Enchantment: The Art of Changing Hearts, Minds, and Actions* at a leadership conference where we were both speaking. In chapter 4, entitled "How to Prepare," Guy talks about conducting *premortems*, a concept created by Gary Klein that Guy read about in the *Harvard Business Review*.[4] The concept of a premortem is similar to one of the processes we used at Wesley College, and the book is well worth the read. According to the research referenced in Klein's article, "Prospective hindsight—imagining that an event has already occurred—increases the ability to correctly identify reasons for future outcomes by 30%. We have used prospective hindsight to devise a method called a premortem, which helps project teams identify risks at the outset."[5] In theory and practicality, when you have the time and resources, this approach is both insightful and beneficial.

The problem when you do not have a robust culture of self-assessment that is practiced and embraced by most within the context of a "process-driven" versus "personality-driven" organization is that you can quickly find that problems are more numerous, much bigger, and more complex than originally realized. Unfortunately, that was the case throughout my first year and a half at Wesley. A positive and effective culture can provide the framework for positive change, but change needs some measure of time and resources to accomplish.

In recent years, many service-oriented industries, as well as other institutions of higher education, have used consolidations, mergers, and acquisitions as a means of consolidating institutional strengths in order to provide more services to a larger population at a more competitive and sustainable cost—in short, providing the best return on investment for services provided. It became apparent the more we dissected Wesley's operational and financial situation that we needed to find a partner who had the financial means for sustainability but lacked some of the in-demand programs we offered at Wesley. These programs included our nursing programs, education programs, and the only Master of Occupational Therapy program in the region. And it was just as apparent, and more time critical, that we find an investor who could provide the financial support required to allow us the time to find our partner.

Changing the State's View on Supporting Higher Education and Securing State Funding

When everything seems to be going against you, remember that the airplane takes off against the wind, not with it.

—HENRY FORD[6]

While we were working to find a long-term partner (which will be discussed later in this chapter), we were in immediate need of a short-to-medium-range solution to our financial and operational short-falls—an investor. That investor was right down the street in the form of the state legislature. It would not be an easy task to convince the state legislature to make a committed investment to Wesley College, but it was a task essential to our survival, and more importantly it was a task critical to the region and higher education in general. We had the opportunity to highlight Wesley's Worth while also changing the narrative regarding the politicians' and public's, at times narrow, view on higher education, which for so long had been binned as "private" or "public" when it came to resource and financial support.

As discussed earlier in this chapter, shortly after arriving at Wesley we would spend several days a week at Legislative Hall engaging with state leadership and their staffs. So, by the time 2018 arrived, we had established a professional relationship with some of the key legislators and their staffs. The access, recognition, and occasional fiscal support up to that point were appreciated and necessary to provide the relevancy and foothold that would be essential in getting substantial and sustainable funding moving forward. As in any courtship, after "friend raising" and small "asks" for support, it was now time to sit down with the head of the company for a formal presentation and "ask"—one that would be transformational rather than merely transactional.

The biggest challenge with the state was being able to convince enough key, and most importantly influential, legislators who were not local of the importance of Wesley College—Wesley's Worth. In the spring of 2019, as we worked to find a long-term partner, we decided to go right to the top. A meeting with the governor was scheduled to lay out our plan and solicit an investment from the state. Wesley had hosted the governor several times at the college, including when he officiated the coin toss at our 2018 homecoming football game, and Wesley's leadership, most notably my board chair and vice chair, had a good professional relationship with him.

My board chair and I entered the governor's office and sat at a small table along with his education advisor, a young man whom we had also established a good professional relationship with and hosted at the college on several occasions. The brief was short and to the point, consisting of six slides summarized in the following list:

- *Exhausting All Sustainability Options*
  - Three bullets breaking down our deficit reduction plan— highlighting the fact that we were not coming to the state as a first option and we were taking "out of hide" first
  - One bullet highlighting our partnership pursuit progress/ status
- *Immediate Need*
  - Graphical representation of our cash flow needs for May– Sept. (our minimal revenue months)
- *Support That Leads to Stability and Growth* (two slides)
  - One in graphic form and one in tabular form, outlining the investment that would be requested over the next five years
- *Wesley's Request of the Governor and State*
  - Two bullets
    - Allow Wesley the privilege to continue providing Delaware students educational opportunities that improve their lives and the communities that they will serve—80% of which are in Delaware
    - Provide state investment to ensure our near-term survivability and long-term sustainability/growth
      - from current-year appropriations, like the Strategic Fund
      - allocated in at least the next five state budgets

- *Wesley's Worth vs. Wesley's Loss*
  - Provided as figure 1, this was the one slide "takeaway" that showed what the investment would ensure, as well as the consequences of not investing

The governor balked at our ask, referencing our status as a "private institution" in spite of our efforts to demonstrate our "public" impact in the state and the future benefit of any investment the state would make. The discussion went back and forth until he asked what the next step was if he could not support our request, at which point we thanked him for his time and consideration and stated that after informing our internal campus community we would hold a press conference in the next month or so announcing the closing of Wesley College. While speaking, the Wesley's Worth slide (figure 1) was placed in front of the governor. There was a noticeable change in the governor's

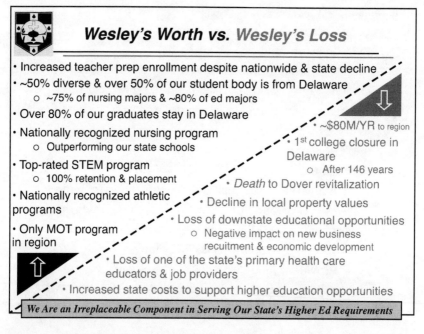

Figure 1. Wesley's Worth vs. Wesley's Loss slide from the March 13, 2019, brief to the Delaware governor.

demeanor, and at that moment Wesley's Worth became clear to him, maybe not holistically, but politically.

Though the meeting ended without a decision, the process that would provide the needed state investment would soon begin, allowing Wesley College time to continue operations and find a partner for long-term sustainability. In addition to providing a path forward for Wesley College, our efforts helped better inform the narrative that higher education in Delaware should not be judged by the arcane binning of schools as "private" or "public" but more aptly by how the institutions serve the state, both in education and post-graduation employment in the state—in short, "return on investment."

The process to eventually secure the appropriated funding was an extremely difficult one, not in terms of meeting well-defined guidelines, which were lacking, but in terms of political posturing levied by a few individuals who manipulated a less than informed "oversight body" to control their own narrative, which at times did not reflect the currency or reality of our situation. Personal feelings had to be set aside, and it was important for us to maintain the "high road" whenever possible. We needed to take the long view to secure a path forward for Wesley College while also helping to change the way state funding for higher education was appropriated.

Throughout the process, we continued to engage with our supportive local, state, and congressional leadership and their staffs on a regular basis, providing status updates on our engagements with the state and courting of a potential partner. Our goal was to stay ahead of any potential uninformed statements in the media, or politically motivated "message spinning," which could have negatively impacted our efforts. By providing biweekly, and at times weekly, updates, as well as periodic in-person meetings, misunderstandings were prevented and our supporters and key decision makers remained informed and engaged.

As a result of our measured efforts and steadfast support of our local state representatives, state senators, and congressional delegation and their staffs, not only was a funding path established for our college, but more importantly a funding line, the Higher Education

Economic Development Investment Fund, was clarified to provide support to all institutions of higher education in the state of Delaware.[7] No binning of "private" and "public," just "return on investment."

Finding and Securing a Partner: Sometimes the Answer Is Closer Than You Thought

We must accept finite disappointment, but never lose infinite hope.

—MARTIN LUTHER KING JR.[8]

In parallel with our efforts to secure long-term state support, we started to actively seek out a partnership. In late 2018, I had a discussion with my board chair about approaching the University of Delaware (UD). We had collaborated with them in myriad areas, and with our downstate presence and renowned health care and teaching programs, we thought that we could provide a smaller, more personal health care–focused branch of a larger state institution. Our idea was something like "the University of Delaware, Wesley College Campus," a similar construct that many other educational systems in other states have adopted: the Penn State distributed campus model, the Rutgers distributed campus model, the University of Wisconsin distributed campus model, and, as already discussed in this book, the University of Tennessee distributed campus model, to name a few. As mentioned early on, every decision made about Wesley had an underpinning of thought regarding the benefit that such a decision would have on our community, state, and region. A partnership with UD would certainly have been beneficial to Wesley College, but it would have been transformational in terms of expanded educational opportunities for our community and downstate. During the next nine months, both institutions conducted some initial due diligence and we hosted campus visits by members of UD's staff. In the end, it was not of interest to UD and no agreements were made, and the courtship ended in early 2019.

Over the next couple years, we would have several potential partners, some that we courted, and others that courted us. Most only made it through the initial discussion phase, and a few involved memorandums of understanding. To help with the process and ensure that our campus community was involved as much as possible with finding, and solidifying, a partnership, we formed a Partnership Advisory Group (PAG) made up of faculty, staff, cabinet members, and at times the Student Government Association (SGA) president. The PAG's size would fluctuate as the task at hand dictated, but it usually involved around 15 individuals. The PAG provided counsel, worked on numerous information pieces, provided data, gave updates as appropriate to the campus community, and became the core of various co-institutional working groups. We all signed nondisclosure agreements to protect the confidentiality of the discussions, and the business-sensitive information that may be shared, until a given process reached the point that public disclosure was warranted.

Throughout the process of seeking a partnership, as well as in all major actions we embarked on at Wesley, the importance of our board of trustees cannot be overstated. Their counsel, engagement, and support were critical in every aspect of the process, including providing financial support to ensure the college could continue operations during one particularly challenging summer.

Shortly after the fall semester started in 2019, while working on a potential partnership with another small local institution, we received a call from an out-of-state university president who wanted to discuss a potential partnership. He explained that his institution was looking at expanding nationally and utilizing established institutions in key regional markets as the mechanism. In theory, it was like what we were looking to do with UD, but on a national, versus state, level. Because we now had two potential opportunities, we enlisted the services of an individual familiar with higher ed mergers and acquisitions on a part-time basis to assist us in balancing the two prospects and aiding our PAG. Our advisor proved beneficial in providing insight into both institutions we were courting and assisting our PAG, and was an influential external advocate for our college.

Not long after the first several meetings, we executed a letter of intent with the out-of-state potential partner as we worked toward a definitive agreement. Over the next seven months, their leadership team made several trips to campus, and their president met, sometimes in person and sometimes on conference calls, with members of our board of trustees, including our board chair, as well as several members of the state legislature, including two political appointees, Delaware's secretary of state and Delaware's director of the Office of Management and Budget.

The out-of-state institution had hired a third-party consultant to help with the due diligence, and in early 2020 we were moving forward with an aggressive timeline. It projected a definitive agreement would be worked out in February, we would meet with the accreditors in March , the out-of-state institution would assist us financially to supplement state support over the summer, and pending accreditation approval would be complete in the spring of 2021. Additionally, around this same time, our other prospect decided not to pursue a partnership with us, and our sole focus became the out-of-state institution. At first, we stayed on task and on schedule, but as February approached there were some process issues that raised red flags. These included timelines slipping, the third-party consultants being our sole point of contact, meetings without representation from the out-of-state institution's leadership team, and their president being less engaged than when we had first started. Concern was voiced about meetings without institutional representation, especially since the third-party consultants had very little higher ed experience, as well as the lack of engagement by the president. We were assured by their president that our concerns would be remedied.

During this same period, the president of Delaware State University (DSU) reached out and expressed an interest in a partnership. We had an initial discussion that included a member of his board of trustees and my board chair. We had known DSU's president long before he came to DSU, and my board chair and one of their board members had known each other for decades and were friends. It became clear that

DSU's president and at least some members of their board had discussed this partnership opportunity, but we, unfortunately had to inform them that we had already signed a letter of intent with an out-of-state institution and were working toward formulating a definitive agreement. They appreciated the candor and wished, as their president would state, that they would have had a chance "at the plate." Understanding our position and restrictions, they planned to do what was necessary to position themselves favorably in case something fell through with the out-of-state institution.

Despite the assurances from the president of the out-of-state institution, as March 2020 arrived, we began experiencing increased delays in achieving a definitive agreement, and major milestones started to slide at an increasing rate. Though some of our out-of-state potential partner's challenges could have been attributed to the COVID-19 pandemic, DSU's leadership was able to get to the place on our execution timeline that we should have been with our potential out-of-state partner, as well as start the draft of a definitive agreement. We did not have the financial stability to continue to go back and forth, and it was critical that we have an agreement before the end of the academic year (July 2020). Waiting for the out-of-state potential partner to get back on track, after showing the inefficiency of their efforts as we got down to making key decisions, seemed a less than optimal path for success. Additionally, DSU's president had made every milestone he said he would, as well as ensured continued state support and support of their board (confirmed through our board-to-board contacts). DSU was a school demographically similar to Wesley, and both our leadership teams had similar values and commitments to the city, state, and region we served. After discussions with the PAG, and then with our board of trustees, we decided to focus our efforts on closing a deal with DSU, rather than continuing with the out-of-state potential partner.

With the impacts of the COVID-19 pandemic starting to be realized nationwide, many institutions were furloughing, laying off, or cutting compensation for faculty and staff. Empathetic for the anxiety and stress affecting our campus community as we worked to finalize a partnership agreement, and with the concerns and uncertainties surrounding COVID-19, we pledged that there would be no furloughs, layoffs, or pay reductions in 2020. The action to preserve our faculty and staff positions and pay proved beneficial. Because of our actions, and relatively small size, we eventually qualified for relief under the Payment Protection Plan (PPP), as part of the Coronavirus Aid, Relief, and Economic Security (CARES) Act. This, in addition to the state support and subsequent Higher Education Emergency Relief (HEER) Funds, provided the critically needed financial stability to help us continue operations through 2021.

Agreement to Acquisition

I have been impressed with the urgency of doing. Knowing is not enough; we must apply. Being willing is not enough; we must do.

—LEONARDO DA VINCI[9]

The initial discussions between DSU's president and myself, along with select members of our leadership teams and boards, discussed the process of exploring Wesley College as the city campus / DIII affiliate (a term first introduced by DSU's chief operating officer) of DSU, with the understanding that the name and functionality could change as we worked through the particulars of the deal. Our immediate focus was to get a definitive agreement drafted and our boards' approval, along with the concurrence of the state, before the end of the academic year—July 2020.

DSU had hired consultants to assist in the drafting of a definitive agreement, as well as to aid in the follow-up process leading to closing the deal. In terms of internal assist, we were slightly ahead, having our PAG already established. DSU would start to formulate a similar group over the summer and into the next year while utilizing their consultants and leadership team to work on the process in the beginning.

On July 9, 2020, after both boards approved, we signed an acquisition agreement (in essence our definitive agreement) with DSU. The agreement was a detailed fifty-four-page document that outlined all aspects and requirements that would be needed to ensure that all actions required for acquisition would be completed by the closing date the following year, July 1, 2021. There would be no change in the operation of Wesley College over the next year, and because of the uncertainties resultant from the COVID-19 pandemic there were some contingencies listed in the acquisition agreement that had to be satisfied to complete the deal. The major contingencies included the following: (1) private and state funding must be secured to cover the acquisition, and (2) the acquisition had to be approved by the Middle States Commission on Higher Education (both institutions' accrediting body), as well as the Department of Education. The acquisition agreement also delineated a process in which through the sale of selective properties (which would belong to DSU after closing), DSU would help Wesley financially for the next year, up to closing. Though the acquisition agreement had a positive effect in that it helped ensure continued state funding and opened foundational interest that provided DSU support, it also publicly announced the transformation of Wesley College, which had a negative impact on our already strained enrollment numbers.

The timeline was extremely aggressive even in a "perfect world," but with COVID-19 many questioned our ability to execute the plan we outlined in the acquisition agreement. Both institutions' leadership teams and board of trustees, as well as our PAG and DSU's eventual transition team, worked tirelessly to ensure that deadlines were met and the process moved forward as efficiently as possible. Our PAG, and our VPF/CFO, in conjunction with DSU's COO and consultants, were in constant communication and on several occasions found opportunities to positively affect the financial bottom line. For example, both institutions used the same IT contractor and same food services contractor. There were definite operational, as well as cost, benefits, to be realized with the consolidation of both contracts post-acquisition and, as was pointed out early on in our discussions, potential financial costs if one or both entities were terminated.

There were regularly scheduled phone calls with DSU's president to discuss any issues or concerns, as well as formulating "messaging"—internal and external—as the process began to unfold. As is the case with all ventures, and especially with one as unique and urgent as ours, there were occasional issues with data dissemination and archiving, as well as distractive missteps that could have negatively impacted our timeline if gone unchecked. Examples of distractive missteps included: decisions being implemented without authority, misrepresentations of presidential directions or intent, and individuals delaying deliverables that were time-critical. Most issues were easily corrected following our phone calls, but it took a concerted effort on both sides to keep folks on task and on time.

Biweekly, or weekly when needed, virtual forums were held to keep the campus community current on the acquisition process, as well as to provide updates related to COVID-19 and to allow for questions and concerns to be raised and addressed. Additionally, biweekly updates were sent to the campus community as well as local, state, and federal leadership and were also posted on our website for widest dissemination. As the transition process progressed, we held joint DSU–Wesley virtual forums, and on several occasions DSU's president came to Wesley to speak with various departments.

An important part of the transition process was ensuring that all our students had the opportunity to continue their education, either at DSU or an institution that better aligned with their needs. Additionally, we made every effort possible to ensure those members of our faculty and staff that were not retained by DSU had the best possible support in finding placement in a desired area that was commensurate with their skills. We provided transition counseling, offered to write letters of recommendation, and made phone calls to help members of our campus community as they transitioned. Many members took advantage of the transition assistance, and several took me up on my offer to personally engage on their behalf, which I gladly did. In fact, during the last few months of my presidency I spent several hours a day either writing letters of recommendation or advocating for a member of my faculty or staff over the phone.

Even today when former colleagues reach out, I provide whatever assistance is needed to help them realize their career desires. Another action worth mentioning is that we issued federal Worker Adjustment and Retraining Notification (WARN) Act alerts, both internally and externally. These are federally mandated notifications that were established for large plant or mass layoffs. It is arguable whether our acquisition qualified for such notifications under the WARN Act, but we decided to leave no doubt and issued them to the appropriate state and local officials, as well as to members of our faculty and staff.

After just over a year of adapting to a catastrophic worldwide pandemic, dealing with some incredible challenges, and in just under a year from signing the acquisition agreement, Wesley College became Wesley College of Health and Behavioral Sciences as part of Delaware State University.

Despite the concerns and anxieties about the future, and a failed lawsuit by a small group of disgruntled faculty members to stop the acquisition, about 60% of our faculty and staff transitioned to DSU. Our students wanting to continue their education found a home, and our campus remained alive to continue to provide the life-changing opportunities for students that it has done for the past 150 years. Mixed opinions remain within the Wesley College family regarding the acquisition, even considering the alarming fact that the closure rate of colleges and universities has drastically increased over the past several years—a trend that unfortunately may continue in the coming years. There are no mixed opinions or debate on the fact that the other option, of becoming a 55-acre plot of boarded-up buildings in downtown Dover, would have been catastrophic for the surrounding area, city, and state.

Reflections

The longing for certainty . . . is in every human mind.
But certainty is generally an illusion.

—OLIVER WENDELL HOLMES[10]

Only time will tell if Delaware State University's acquisition of Wesley College and its subsequent transformation to the Wesley College of Health and Behavioral Sciences will provide the increase in educational opportunities to our state and region, as well as a catalyst for the revitalization of downtown Dover, that those who supported the acquisition had envisioned. I am hopeful that it will, but history, not us, will be the final judge.

If Wesley College had taken a different approach decades ago, would we still be an independent institution today? We will never know, but I believe a partnership would have been inevitable as the higher education landscape continues to shrink and evolve. We cannot change history, but we do have the opportunity to affect the future, and the discussions you have today will allow for a more measured approach to your future.

Unlike Wesley College, you may have the opportunity for an understanding early on of what may be needed in your future for sustainability and relevance. If you have that opportunity, seize it by formulating a plan of action, should it be needed in the future. Your informed proactivity will ensure that if, or more than likely when, change is warranted, you will have the time and resources to ensure equity and leverage in a partnership that will expand the opportunities to the students and communities you serve.

Notes

1. Jack Welch Quotes. GoodReads.com. Retrieved June 24, 2022, from https://www .goodreads.com/author/quotes/3770.Jack_Welch.

2. Chip Heath and Dan Heath. 2010. *Switch: How to Change Things When Change Is Hard* (New York: Broadway Books).

3. John F. Kennedy Quotes. InternetPoems.com. Retrieved June 24, 2022, from https:// internetpoem.com/john-f-kennedy/quotes/change-is-the-law-of-life-and-those-who -look-only-35298/.

4. Guy Kawasaki. 2011. *Enchantment: The Art of Changing Hearts, Minds, and Actions* (New York: Portfolio/Penguin).

5. Gary Klein. 2007. "Performing a Project Premortem," *Harvard Business Review*, September, https://hbr.org/2007/09/performing-a-project-premortem.

6. Henry Ford. SetQuotes.com. Retrieved June 24, 2022, from https://www.setquotes.com /when-everything-seems-to-be-going-against-you-airplane-against-wind/.

7. "Governor Carney's FY 2020 Budget." Retrieved June 24, 2022, from https://governor .delaware.gov/fy20budget/.

8. Holly Lebowitz Rossi. "Martin Luther King, Jr. on 'Infinite Hope.'" Guideposts.com. Retrieved June 24, 2022, from https://www.guideposts.org/inspiration/inspiring -stories/stories-of-hope/martin-luther-king-jr-on-infinite-hope.

9. Maricel Cabahug. 2017. "The Urgency of Doing." LinkedIn.com, April 27. https://www .linkedin.com/pulse/urgency-doing-maricel-cabahug.

10. Debbie Bianucci. 2020. "Three Key Factors for Effective 2021 Planning in Financial Services." Forbes.com, December 4. https://www.forbes.com/sites /forbesfinancecouncil/2020/12/04/three-key-factors-for-effective-2021-planning-in -financial-services/?sh=63c4817621df.

Conclusion
Common Lessons

———

IT HAS BEEN said that if you have seen one merger . . . well . . . then . . . you have seen one merger, and that the only consistency is inconsistency. There is no one process, let alone an instructional checklist, that will ensure a merger's success. In fact, there is no singular definition of success. Instead, we are invited to learn from the experiences of those who have gone before us. The authors in this book have generously shared their stories in hopes that the lessons learned will provide a valuable reference for those seeking to maintain and sustain their particular and invaluable mission in higher education. In the process of compiling these stories, several common learnings became evident.

A Clear and Shared Sense of Mission

The more your various constituencies are aligned in their understanding of your institution's mission the better. Different stakeholder groups will experience the mission in unique ways, but the following questions will assist in solidifying those understandings:

Why are we here? Who do we serve? What would be lost if we were to cease operation? What would be missing? How will it affect our community, economy, accessibility to higher ed, workforce development, and so on?

Alumni are more likely to understand the mission as they experienced it at the time they attended the institution. For instance, if your four-year institution that now has a student body that is more than 50% Pell Grant–eligible and first-generation college students once was a junior college and predominantly white and middle class, then your alumni will remember the institution that way and may see it from that perspective. The alumni of the junior college will need to know that the mission of the institution has adapted to the needs of a changing world and the impact that these changes in mission are making in the community and world.

Faculty and staff may understand the institution's mission as they prefer it or wish it to be. Those with a long-standing relationship with the institution may still see the mission as it was 20 or 30 years ago, rather than recognizing the institution's response to the changing needs of students and communities. Questions like the following will help faculty and staff ground themselves in the present and future mission of the institution: How do we serve the students that we accept and how do we prepare them to serve the world's needs today? What is the role of the liberal arts core? How do we apply technology and new ways of operating to meet the needs of students who are living and working in a technology-rich world?

A clear and shared sense of mission is the essential foundation for making decisions that have the power to preserve, sustain, expand, or enhance the enterprise.

Sustainability and Effectiveness of Mission Is the Top Priority

Accomplishing the agreed-upon mission in a sustainable and more effective manner must be primary in our strategic thinking and planning. Identity and preferred ways of operating and programming are important parts of accomplishing the institution's mission, but they are impossible to maintain without financial stability. A truly sustainable institution not only balances its budget year to year but also provides the educational resources necessary to serve the students they accept. A sustainable institution budgets for deferred maintenance, has a prudent endowment spending policy, and provides cost-of-living compensation increases to its employees. As Martin Methodist College examined its financial state in the light of what it truly means to be sustainable, there was a realization that though we could keep our head above water our students needed more than that, our staff and faculty deserved more than that, and the needs of our region required more than we could offer.

Historically, higher education has been known for incrementalism and the glacial pace of change. Transformational change requires a strong sense of urgency. Leaders are responsible for creating a shared sense of urgency around the real threats and realistic opportunities surrounding their institutions.

As the president of Montreat College, Paul Mauer, argues, today's college president needs to be more than a CEO—they must also be the chief urgency officer (CUO). Without creating a sense of urgency, leaders will not create the buy-in and support required to accomplish meaningful change.

Not a Last Resort

Without question, the most important common lesson is that the time to contemplate any form of merger is before it becomes a last resort. When one comes to the table as a last resort, it creates a critical power imbalance that leaves the institution at a distinct disadvantage in any negotiation. Waiting until the institution is on the brink of failure can also severely limit the field and quality of both potential partners and potential positive outcomes. One piece of advice that rose to the top in each and every merger story was this: early and frank discussions while you have the means and time to ensure relevance, equity, and leverage will provide your institution with the best opportunity for success. A successful merging strategy must be mission-driven rather than survival-driven. In fact, merger can come about organically as an institution thinks strategically about how to accomplish its mission when it actively views partnership, collaboration, and merger as strategic tools.

Not a Failure

One of the potential obstacles to seeing merger as a strategic tool lies in seeing a merger as a failure or as giving up the struggle that our institutions somehow manage to win year after year. However, when we employ mission-minded thinking, any opportunity to sustain and grow that mission is a win. Merging is not failure; rather, the failure is found in refusing to take action in the face of trends that clearly predict mission failure or compromise.

Though it's always important to celebrate short-term wins, doing so without seriously considering long-term sustainability creates a false sense of security. Accomplishing something that can preserve, sustain, expand, and enhance your mission long term is a great triumph that requires courageous leadership that is willing to advance the mission strategically, wherever that leads.

Success Is Relative

The measures of success in any merger are relative to the unique circumstances precipitating the merger and the preferred outcomes for each party. In some cases, a merger is seeking to accomplish something positive from dire and negative circumstances. In the case of Wesley College, the parties were able to maintain a thriving campus facility and preserve a number of valuable programs now under the administration of Delaware State University. Valuable and tangible missional assets were preserved on what is now the Wesley College of Health & Behavioral Sciences.

Failure to merge can lead to successful outcomes. The process of considering and evaluating whether a merger is the right strategy can help more clearly define an institution's mission and the elements of its culture that are important to preserve. It can also result in a whole new sense of appreciation for a mission that was otherwise taken for granted. The process of considering and evaluating a merger can lead to broadening a team's vision and revealing formerly unseen opportunities. When the board of trustees at Point University voted to discontinue efforts to merge with Montreat College, it was not the beginning of the end but a "near-death" experience that would become a platform for urgent change. When the college received a lifeline from a miracle gift, President Maurer knew that part of the stewardship of this miracle was to urgently lead the college to examine its business model, recast its mission, and make changes that would lay claim to who they uniquely are and better respond to the needs of the world they serve. Maurer and the leadership came to a paradigm-shifting realization that they were a 100-year-old "start-up." Seeing itself as a start-up changed the way the college operated, made decisions, and envisioned its future. With its first operational surplus in many years, the college is beginning to experience a healthy fiscal position.

Due Diligence

Do your due diligence before engaging a potential merger partner. Are they, or have they been, involved in other potential mergers? Can they demonstrate the support of their board, administration, faculty, and staff, or is the desire to explore merging only firmly held by their president and a handful of administrators? Do they truly value what you bring to the table and is what they bring valuable to your mission? Are they financially secure and in good stead with their regional accreditor? In addition to asking these questions of potential partners, it is important to be aware of your own institution's answers.

It is crucial to count the cost. Mergers are expensive and require a large outlay of resources. There are expenses that come with the use of various consultants, lawyers, public relations professionals, appraisers, and other professionals. In addition to monetary expenses, there is a necessity to devote a large amount of staff time and energy in the process.

In doing your due diligence, regional accreditors, federal and state departments, regulators, commissions, and affiliated church bodies cannot be an afterthought. Connect with these entities at the outset of your discussions and become well versed in the timelines, guidelines, and submission requirements for each. Any of these entities can derail, delay, disrupt, or even destroy your plan if not properly considered and satisfied. Iowa Wesleyan discovered far into its attempt to merge with Saint Leo University that by transferring its governance to a Florida school, their students would no longer qualify for the Iowa Tuition Grant. Martin Methodist College discovered that their USDA loan could not transfer to a public entity. The University of Tennessee would be required to refinance this debt. This added additional complexity to the process.

Nonnegotiables

Prior to launching a search for a partner to enter into a merger discussion with, it is vital to compile a list of your institution's "non-negotiables." Preserving the mission is likely at the top of that list. Are there items related to identity and operational structure that the administration, board, students, or community are absolutely unwilling to give up? It is important to identify those up front. Survey various constituencies to see what they consider negotiable. Ask questions such as: Is changing the historic name acceptable? Is there an acceptable level of workforce reduction? Is retiring the institution's board and high-level executives acceptable? This all begins with an initial set of terms and agreements. These terms and agreements will necessarily change throughout the process, but set a crucial framework of expectations. The St. Andrews leadership made it a goal that the college's name, identity, mission, church-relatedness, and separate corporate existence be maintained to the greatest extent possible. For Wheelock College, the leadership engaged the community to set out a list of low-, medium-, and high-level priorities in their negotiations. At the same time, Mary Churchill maintains that the school must position itself as an attractive partner.

A true negotiation cannot take place unless both parties are trying to achieve a goal with the understanding that compromise will be necessary to achieve an acceptable outcome. There has to be "something in it" for each institution. The merger should have the potential to enhance the mission of all parties, creating a mutually beneficial outcome. Each institution needs to believe that they bring something valuable to the table. If the balance of power tilts too heavily toward one party, the merger becomes more of a takeover and can lead quickly to poor morale and resentment.

Culture Matters

No two institutions share the exact same cultures. There can be differences in forms of governance and structure. An institution can be public or private, have primarily commuter or residential students, have a liberal arts core or not, use a tenure system or not, have a religious or secular foundation, be primarily socially conservative or liberal in values, or highly value diversity, equity, and inclusion or homogeneity. Culture matters, and merging cultures is a difficult task. Encouragingly, cultures can and do unite successfully, but it is important to take into consideration that some assimilation and acculturation are a part of the process for both merging cultures. Often, one institution has a more dominant culture in one area, while the other institution has a more dominant culture in another. Recognizing these differences and addressing their implications from the beginning will address fears, rational or irrational, and inform your planning and negotiations. When a private institution becomes a campus of a public system, it has real implications both positive, in terms of resources, and challenging, in terms of added bureaucracy and politics. Being a state institution means being subject to the state legislature, constitutional officers, and a number of state commissions.

Honor the Legacy

In the process of seeking an alternative future, it is important to know and respect the history of the institution. Engage those within the institution who are the keepers of history and culture. Long-standing faculty, staff, alumni, emeritus faculty, and members of the broader community can help link a revered past to a promising future. At Martin Methodist, honoring the past meant realizing that the history of preserving mission required many adaptations in the past, including becoming coeducational, moving from a junior college to a senior college, and the changing of the name of the institution. The move that was being contemplated was just the next chapter in a long history of adaptation that had already spanned 150 years. Martin Methodist also found ways to celebrate and honor the past while moving into the future. A picnic was held on the college green and faculty emeriti shared precious memories and humorous stories. Figures that played a prominent role in the first 150 years were commemorated in the naming of spaces and programs that would transfer to the new identity. The seal of the new institution would bear marks of tradition, including the iconic columns that became a brand marking for the college. As a college of the United Methodist Church, a worship service was held with a theme of remembering the past and embracing the future.

Transparency and Trust

Transparency and trust are the bedrock of all healthy institutions. They are important when seeking partnerships and collaborations, but absolutely essential in a merger. The board of trustees, faculty, and staff deserve a full picture of the state of the college and the strengths, weaknesses, opportunities, and threats before them. Accurate data from trusted sources must be made available so they can serve as the foundation to inform and motivate decision-making. Make it a goal to reach conclusions based on data rather than on one's opinion or preferences. Be sure that all actions are documented so there are no hidden agendas or under-the-table dealings.

If transparency and trust seems like a tall order, you are not alone. In order to bring about transformational change, it is often necessary to change the institutional culture. Many years of struggling and just getting by can lead to low morale, a survival mentality, and a lack of agency and ownership. Developing a coalition of the willing through transparency, honest assessment of the circumstances, and authentic empowerment can lift an institution above the malaise to a realistic and more hopeful place where an authentic sense of agency is restored. As a leader in your institution, you can begin the necessary cultural shift through your own transparency.

In our first story of Wheelock College and Boston University, Mary Churchill stressed the importance of quality leadership. The leadership that their team aspired to would include a combination of characteristics and practices ascribed to "servant" and "authentic" leadership styles. These characteristics and practices included transparency, self-awareness, shared decision-making, multiple communication channels, and open listening sessions. Leadership must be more than transactional, says Churchill. Leaders must communicate honestly and transparently, and honor the institution's history.

When dealing with a merger partner, you will find that many of the terms and agreements that are negotiated are more covenantal than binding and legal. Trusting that the partner will honor their covenants to the best of their ability is a necessary part of the process.

Critical Communication

Controlling the narrative around the institution's circumstances both within the institution and in its surrounding community is vitally important. Sharing accurate and timely information builds trust, reduces misunderstandings, and dismisses counternarratives. Communication also has the power to build the positive momentum necessary to overcome the natural resistance to transformational change that is a part of what it means to be human. Sharing all the information you can, when you can, reduces anxiety even when the information is very challenging and threatens change. Mablene Kruger, former president of Robert Morris University Illinois, helped set the narrative by naming the merger information page "Building a Stronger University." She maintains that the president must become the chief cheerleader for the prospective merger. Both presidents of RMUI and Roosevelt University were careful to define the merger as an integration rather than an assimilation. This defined and helped set the tone for the work ahead.

Considerations regarding athletics must be front and center. With athletics playing such a prominent role in our institutions, it is necessary to communicate early and often. At Martin Methodist College, many of the first questions asked after the merger process announcement related to concerns about the future of athletics. Second only to, "Will I still have a job?"

While there is no instructional checklist that will ensure a merger's success, a lot can be learned from the experiences of the colleges and universities in this book. When institutions focus on their mission and vision, consider merger not as a last resort or failure, and prioritize sustainability, effectiveness, culture, transparency, and communication, they can accomplish great things.

INDEX